ALL THAT I WAS

For Kate, who heard it all first and asked me to write it down.

ALL THAT I WAS

A Village Childhood in the Thirties

Eric Austen

All THAT I WAS

Published in 1996 by
Mousehold Press, 6 Constitution Opening
Norwich, NR3 4BD

Cover design by Terry Loan

Illustrations by Eric Austen

ISBN 1 874739 07 2

Printed by Watkiss Studios Ltd., Biggleswade

Who may regret what was, since it has made
Himself himself? All that I was I am,
And the old childish joy now lives in me
At sight of a green field or a green tree.

John Freeman
All that I was I am

Contents

Foreword

Memoirs of childhood appear remarkably often today and especially those about working-class childhoods, urban or rural. Almost all of them are intrinsically interesting. What has inspired these people – many of them, incidentally, retired academics – to sit down and recall their lives of 60 or 70 years ago? Perhaps the rise of oral history is one source. Another and deeper impulse may be the realisation at this point in their lives of how far they have travelled physically and in spirit; of how much more complex and bewildering is the world of today; of how childhood had a human scale and some apparently immutable certainties.

We each bring our special and, until the moment of writing, often unrecognised gifts to the self-imposed but unevadable task. Eric Austen brings a particularly strong and still almost childlike sense of wonder, and this sharpens his powers of ordered observation. So does his strong sense of smell. That is not uncommon: George Orwell had it; it is a prime gateway to the 'thisness' of things.

These authors almost always acknowledge the ways their teachers of English awakened their childhood imaginations (as the man called 'M. N. D.' by his pupils does here). Good English teachers recognise their power, their at bottom moral power, and do not abuse it: a touching final visit to M. N. D. in his old people's home towards the end of this book implicitly celebrates this gift.

The better, that is the more self-aware, autobiographers delve deep, even though that sometimes hurts, as when Eric Austen notes his compulsion with tidying up. Freud had an explanation, of course. Since I share that preoccupation I think I can locate in myself its source: you are still trying to put order in, to control, a world which is changing all round you but which you know you must learn to handle if you are going to fulfil what is latent, against many odds.

Almost all such writers have good anecdotes to tell. The most interesting go further and muse long over those incidents. What do they represent, tell, indicate, symbolise? A fine example here is the discovery of the seed potato, used up, sucked dry, cast aside – its biological purpose fulfilled. That gives rise to a meditation on the way we are all caught up in the same process: the vision of his paternal grandmother who had produced fourteen children is called up by that spent potato. It is a haunting moment.

At the back of that reflection on the inevitable sadness and cost of so much of our quotidian life there lies also, just as powerfully, the sense that some virtues remain. Here: in the midst of continuous hardship is the assertion of continuing love. It is often hard today, and as our shadows lengthen, to believe that 'what will survive of us is love'. Recollections of this kind can reinforce that hope.

Richard Hoggart

A pond full of ducks is just around the corner…

WORDS TO BEGIN WITH

Nearing my life's evening, or possibly its late afternoon, I find myself drawn towards reflecting upon the long-gone days of my childhood. I suspect that the pattern of all my later years was mysteriously laid down in that dawn time. I hope now to clarify some of the earliest happenings and perhaps to understand some aspects of my life a little better.

I have become increasingly curious about how others, particularly some whom I know well and love, have become the way they are now. What constellations of events and influences have combined to create the essential self-hood which they as adults live? In my own case, the question is whether I can actually find the origins of various meanings of my life in certain episodes of my childhood.

I am, in the end, as is everyone, faced with the great aloneness of being in the world with unique individual responses, yet I imagine that, unless I am absurdly eccentric, my particular set of memories will have sufficient of the common human experience to justify sharing them.

What follows is a series of sketches and impressions rather than a straight chronological account. The action therefore tends to flit from one scene to another, dallying back and forth. In amongst it all are occasional musings from my adult self on the possible long-term effects of some of the happenings.

Because I am giving this account in my seventieth year the perspective gets shifted – rather like looking through the wrong end of a long telescope. But although the view from where I am now is a long-distance one, I hope it has a particular clarity in spite of being so far away in time. The point of recording it now is that age sometimes plays havoc with the senses and the memory. Advancing years might also find me having lost enthusiasm for the project. So it has to be now or never.

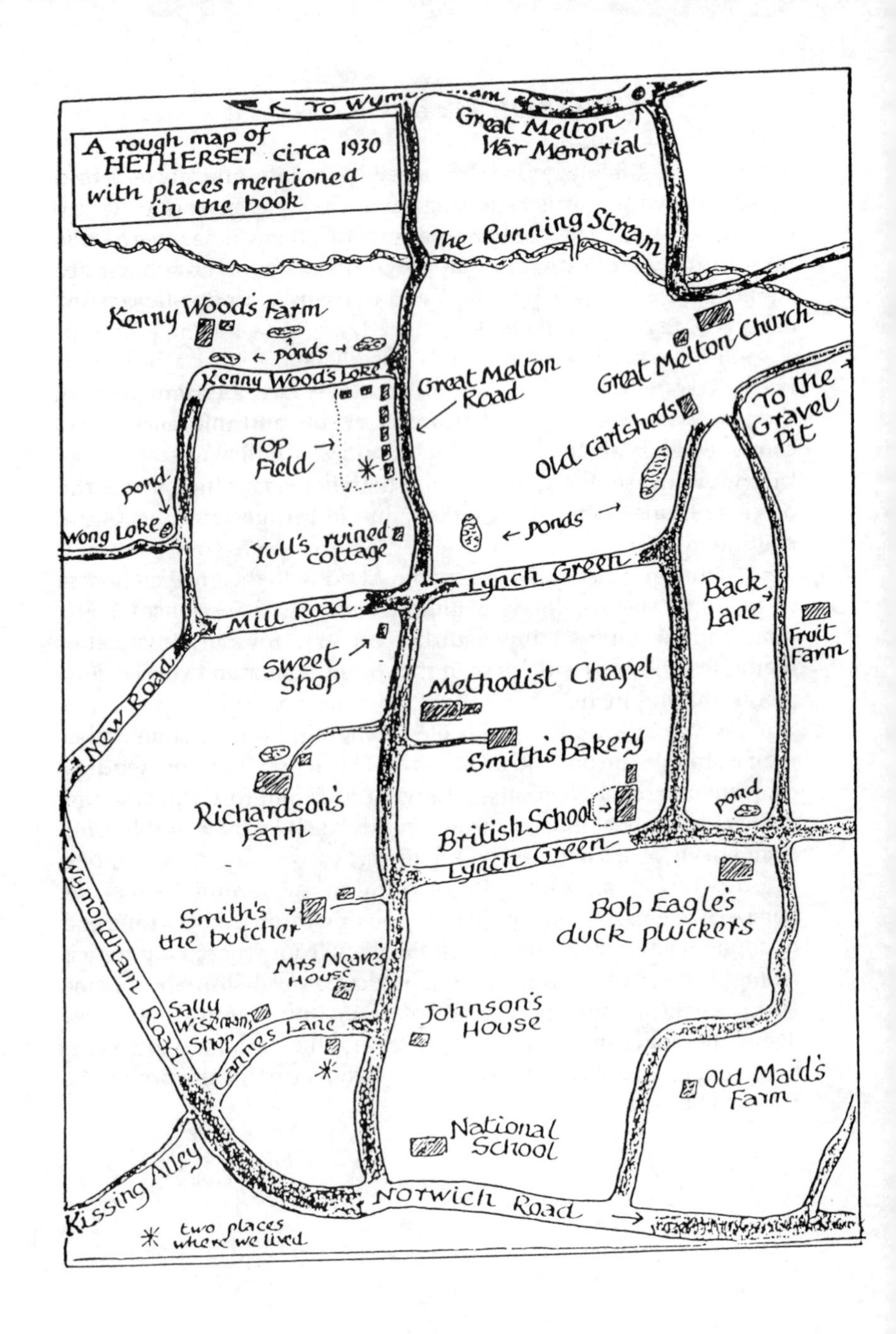
A rough map of HETHERSET circa 1930 with places mentioned in the book
To Wymondham
Great Melton War Memorial
The Running Stream
Kenny Wood's Farm
ponds
Kenny Wood's Loke
Great Melton Road
Great Melton Church
To the Gravel Pit
Old cartsheds
Top Field
pond
Wong Loke
ponds
Yull's ruined cottage
Lynch Green
Back Lane
Mill Road
Fruit Farm
Sweet Shop
New Road
Methodist Chapel
Smith's Bakery
Richardson's Farm
British School
pond
Lynch Green
Wymondham Road
Bob Eagle's duck pluckers
Smith's the butcher
Mrs Neave's House
Sally Wiseman's Shop
Cannes Lane
Johnson's House
Old Maid's Farm
National School
Kissing Alley
Norwich Road
two places where we lived

WHERE IT WAS

My growing up happened in the small Norfolk village of Hethersett which, at that time, had a population of about 1,000 souls.

Hethersett is not to be confused with places like Letheringsett, Stradsett or Tattersett – not the same at all: Hethersett has a much friendlier sound. The original name is recorded in the Domesday Book: it is believed the word Hederseta perhaps meant 'a fold for deer'.

I could just as well have grown up in Great Snoring or even Little Snoring. I could have spent my childhood in Bittering or in Seething, possibly in Wendling. Norfolk is full of hamlets and villages with strange, evocative names. There is Stratton Strawless, Barnham Broom, Quarles, Quidenham, Trunch, and two names so alike as to cause confusion, Tottington and Tuttington. The East Anglian map is alive with such names.

They probably all had the usual village attributes – a church, a chapel, a pub or two, a school, and a village hall, together with a few shops. But they also had, I suspect, the right conditions for nurturing a country childhood – trees and fields, hedges and ditches, duck-ponds and running streams, valleys and hills, back lanes and alleyways, and a good supply of haystacks.

These things Hethersett had in sufficient proportions to provide a background against which I could develop. Added to that it was, in the 1930s, a farming village. The records for the time state: 'The chief crops are wheat, barley, turnips and beetroot and some of the land in pasture.'

My home, then, was on the edge of this village. From our windows we had good views of the changing crops on the opposite fields. Sixty years later the fields are still the same shape, the Running Stream is still at the bottom of the hill and a pond full of ducks is just around the corner.

EARLIEST MEMORIES

Daisy Chains

At the edge of my earliest memories is a summer day. I am three or four years old. I am in a grassy field, full of small white daisies. My mother is there. My sister is there, together with older loving people. We make daisy chains – well, at least, they are making daisy chains. I gape in wonder and surprise as each flower's centre is pierced by a metal knitting needle. Through the hole goes the tiny green stalk of the plucked flower. Thirty or so joined up daises now hang around my neck – nature's first necklace. We all pluck more daisies and place them in somebody's up-turned hat. The sun is shining brightly, the grass is green and dry enough to roll in but not too tall to hide the early summer daisies. There are so many daisies, so abundant are they, that however many we pick they will not be missed on that bright, summer day.

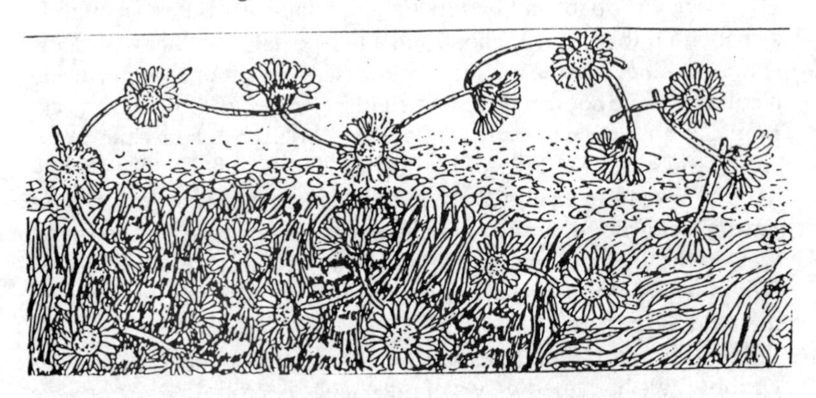

Jam Roly-poly

I am indoors during my fourth year but it is now winter. I kneel on a rag-rug before a wooden armchair. My elbows are leaning on the seat, my hands are around my chin. I look towards the bright fire burning in the soot-filled chimney place. Mother has promised to make me a jam roly-poly pudding. She has mixed the flour and suet, rolled the mixture out flat with her wooden rolling pin. She spreads the plum jam across the flat oblong shape before rolling the pudding into a cylinder. Wrapped into a white linen cloth and tied at both ends with string, it now goes into a very large black saucepan to be boiled. The saucepan stands on the hob over the yellow and red flames of a wood and coal fire. I watch the flames licking round the black shape and the smoke going up the chimney. The waiting is long but it is not, I think, a hungry wait. My sister is away in school, my father is away working on the farm, but what really matters is that she has granted my wish for the pudding. There is the feeling that this is a simple gift from Mum to me alone. The jam roly-poly becomes a symbol of her love for me. There is the fire, the water, the food and the love. But the strongest of all these is the love.

The Christmas Robin

I am now six. It is Christmas. We have moved to a different house. A chocolate-log cake is on the table. It is shaped and decorated to resemble a small tree-trunk. Perched at one end of it is a snowman and, at the other, a robin red-breast. My sister wants the snowman and I have asked for the robin. A few days later, when all the cake has been eaten, our wishes are granted.

It is snowing hard outside: I have my robin redbreast in my hand. I climb into the ditch by the garden hedge. I know that, here, there is last year's birds' nest with its mossy inside still intact. There I will place my little Christmas robin. It will be warm away from the winter winds, frosts and snow. I shall keep an eye on this bird.

This plaster robin is more to me than the real robins that hop and fly about in the garden. I can never catch one of those, they go so fast.

When, as an adult, I reflect upon this scene, I surmise that there began a realisation that symbols of things can have great value. My interest in collecting discarded objects began there. Even now something which I have found and rescued from a skip, or at a tip, or in a jumble sale, can become a trophy, a collector's piece, or an art object. All bring me the same happiness as the sight of the Christmas robin installed in the vacant nest in the winter of 1928.

The Paper Farm

I am still six and it is still winter. My sister is with me on another rag-rug before another fire. We are playing with the simplest toys of our own making. Single sheets of stiffish paper have been doubled over. On one side we have drawn in pencil the shapes of farm animals so that the top part of each one comes where the crease of the paper is. We cut the animal shapes out with scissors, unfold them a little at the feet, so that they will stand up. We arrange our creations into farmyards: sheep in pens, pigs in styes, cows in pastures, horses by stables and ducks in ponds. We survey the scene with satisfaction and pleasure. Suddenly our mother opens the door from the kitchen. Wind from the backyard blows through, scattering our flimsy herds. They are down on their sides, on their backs with legs in the air. Our ducks are drowning in their pond. But we do not complain. We set to and make a new arrangement. All the folded animals are put back on their folded feet. Order comes out of chaos. Was our activity, I wonder, a forerunner of future struggles against great odds? We stoic child-farmers faced howling gales but would never be cast down.

Grandma Symonds

Grandma lived to be 100. Her living may have had little effect on the world at large but her being profoundly affected her small circle of relatives. Numerous cats, a dog or two, many chickens, and a succession of gardens full of flowers, vegetables and herbs all lived under her gentle hand. Amongst this assortment I too thrived.

Grandma was born in October 1880. She was 40 in the year that I was born. Mum and Dad were both aged 22. No doubt Grandma would have been staying in what my parents called our 'titty-totty' cottage in the Norfolk village where they then lived. Grandma, I think, supervised my coming into the world.

My first real memories of her belong to my seventh year. She and Grandad lived, at that time, in a converted railway carriage on a plot of land six miles from our home. After the First World War, perhaps as part of the 'Homes for Heroes' programme, redundant railway carriages could be purchased from Norwich Railway Station for £25 each. Grandad bought one, had it towed to a plot of land in Costessey, mounted it on pieces of chestnut tree-trunks and proceeded to make a home of it. By the time my sister and I had come to stay for a short holiday a transformation had taken place. The inside walls had linings of thin plywood, the floors were carpeted, and the windows were curtained in red and white gingham. Batteries provided little lights in each compartment. We, in our innocent days, had never travelled by train, though we had completed jigsaw puzzles of The Flying Scotsman. Trains were magic things that whistled through the daisy meadows of our earliest childhood. But to travel motionless in our own little beds, through the night of owl-hooting darkness, with Grandma and Grandad gently snoring next-door, this was more than magic.

Grandad mounted it on pieces of chestnut tree trunks …

Grandad Symonds was a cabinet-maker by trade so he had been able to build on to the railway carriage a living room and a kitchen. The place exuded the sweet smell of newly sawn pinewood, as fresh cupboards, shelving and windows were added to the home. In the kitchen was a huge, black, cast-iron cooking range. Grandma stoked the fiery furnace of this veritable engine for the production of endless dumplings, toad-in-the-holes, rice puddings and bread-and-butter puddings. But every morning the ash had to be bucketed away and the monster had to be blackened and polished so that it shone like The Flying Scotsman. This Grandma did.

She had lots of long hair. She was tall and when dressed to go out, she walked just like Queen Mary – everybody said so. Her hair was bundled up high. She wore Queen Mary hats when we went to the city. It was in regard to her putting on her hat that one of my earliest childhood confusions occurred. I remember the great, long hat-pin which she carefully manipulated from left to right through the hat. I firmly believed that the hat-pin went right through her head, somehow to anchor the hat in position for confronting the wind and the rain. Being a shy and rather timid boy I never asked her, never indeed asked anybody, not my sister, nor my mother, nor my father. It seemed to me to be the most reasonable explanation, the way she seemed painstakingly to be digging round with the point of the hat-pin, searching for the hole in her head, to get it right and have no hurt. All this added to my vision of her magical qualities.

In the early thirties and during the Great Slump national newspapers offered coupons which, if saved up and sent off with some cash, enabled families to purchase mass-produced books at cheaper rates. These offers led Grandma to work more magic on me. Having observed that I was a thoughtful, serious boy, at the age of eight given to reading, she decided to buy, over the period of a year or two, I think twelve volumes called *The Wonderland of Knowledge*, illustrated children's encyclopaedias. Each one came in a strong cardboard box. They had blue embossed covers with the number of the volume in gold on the spine – blue and gold are still amongst my favourite colours. I have an old photograph of myself sitting on a little wooden stool, wearing a cap too large for my head. On my lap is a volume of *The Wonderland of Knowledge*. I am gazing out in wonder.

These books really had Grandma's touch. They left the school primers way behind – *Kitty and Rover*, *Chicken Licken* and *Turkey Lurkey* were left standing at the post. *Little Half-Chick* was flattened. For these books were not books, they were volumes and they spoke volumes. I can see their pages now. Fables, Greek myths, the seven wonders of the world, the human body and its wonders – a diagram purporting to show how messages got from the ear to the brain, and from there to the fingers or toes. Little imaginary men running up and down, and all over the body 'Left toe quick march!' they ordered, 'Right-hand fingers scratch head!' they commanded. It was hat-pins in heads again for me and I never looked back.

But there was a hidden bonus which accompanied being a Wonderland reader. Maybe this was not part of Gran's intention. A Wonderland reader, if he was young and artful, got out of helping with household chores if he kept his eyes down on the books.

'Leave him! Can't you see he's reading?' Mum would say and my poor sister would groan off to do the washing up. Grandma, without realising it, had vouchsafed me an 'excused duties permit' which served me well through later life. The grammar school homework was regularly stretched from six o'clock until ten o'clock. Distant chatter of crockery and cutlery from the kitchen pained me not at all. Take books and dazzle the others with your search for knowledge, and you can get anywhere. No one ever caught me with comics or magazines – such reading didn't get you off kitchen duties. It had to be heavy, purposeful material. Today I use philosophy, poetry or psychology. This trio is guarantied to keep the domestic pressure at bay, at least temporarily.

Dear Grandma, how I loved you as a child, how I still love you though you are almost nowhere save in this head that you blessed and smiled on in the long, long past.

'God has forgotten to call me' she often said in her later years. In the mind's eye, I saw a boating lake with numbered boats: 'come in number 99, your time is up' – a flurry of oars and a hurrying to the shore. During those final years it took many hands to 'service' her as we used to call it. My mother, Grandma's daughter, herself already 75 years old, would cycle round to bring clean laundry. My sister, already 55, would go in and warm up Grandma's breakfast of Ambrosia rice pudding. Myself, I was often asked to warm up her false teeth of a winter's morning, while Donald, my brother-in-law, looked in last thing at night. Uncle George, her son, would bring newspapers. Lucy, his wife, would bring shopping items from the city, lights for the cat called Stingy, and sausages for Gran. Grandma was a great survivor. She looked after herself and if that wasn't enough she charmed the rest of us to join in. Because of her particular personality she was rewarding to 'do' for.

The youngish warden of the sheltered accommodation where she lived at the age of 90 conversed with her daily through the two-way communication system. Grandma grew fond of him. In confidence, she asked Kate, my wife, one day when we were on a visit: 'Kate, my dear, what does the word "affinity" mean?' Kate explained as best she could. 'I think,' announced Grandma, 'that I have an affinity with the warden and, do you know, my dear, I think he has one with me. But don't you say anything to the rest of the family, I beg you. You know how they are.' We did know so we didn't say. But we understood just how it came about that dear, lovable, aged Gran had lost a bit of her heart to the warden. The two-way communication system took on a special significance – platonic, innocent, mutual affinity.

We all tried to persuade her to live to be 100. The Queen, we said, will send a telegram, especially for you, in a golden envelope. I thought of the boating lake again but this time 'Come in number 100, your telegram is here.' I knew that Grandma would stay in her boat and land at her own good time. The Queen would no doubt be scanning a large volume of names and dates, her royal pen in her hand. Of course that isn't how it happens. But in 1980 the telegram really came. The mayor came to the party in the old folks' home. A large cake came, photographers came. The family were there and helped to eat up the cake. But old Stingy, her last loved cat, was no longer alive to lick up the crumbs. 'Cat number 16, your time is up! Put down that mouse and swim for the shore!'

PASSING THE TIME

I remember sunny days when even the small lawn was big enough for my sister Irene and me to create a little world. This was achieved with two wooden clothes-horses, an old blanket or two, a worn-out sheet, a couple of cushions, together with other domestic throw-outs from the kitchen. The project was house-building, home-making, camping, all in one. It all had to be our size, not the adult proportions. The snugness and semi-darkness made for mystery. Just to get in there and sit in it, and look down at the grass and up at the blanket, and out through the tiny entrance was rapture. To do only that was a great delight. Eating little snacks and sipping little drinks in this tiny residence completed the illusion of home. We played our childish version of adults' reality for hours on end, never tiring of using our play objects to create this world. Did we want to grow up and join their world? Were we in rehearsal for that or did this game represent the limit of our horizon – was it all that we really knew well?

The heat was overpowering on hot summer mornings and afternoons. One day I actually fainted away and my sister fetched Mum to drag me from under the clothes-horses, and into the fresh air where I recovered. I think that the claustrophobia which gave me many problems later in life began that day on the lawn. It was the first time I had fainted – perhaps nearly died – in our do-it-ourselves miniature home.

Playing with the neighbourhood children consisted of numerous activities. There was hop-scotching, wheeling of wooden hoops, skipping with ropes, spinning of tops, all on the empty roads at our end of the village. Down at the Running Stream we fished for 'tiddlers' with little nets, jam jars and bent pins. We built dams to block the water, and we sailed our paper boats through and under the low road bridge which spanned the Running Stream.

In spring we gathered primroses, cowslips and bluebells in the nearby meadows. In September we picked blackberries for Mum to make jam, and blackberry-and-apple pies. We found hazel-nuts or cobnuts as we called them, picked them and cracked them between our teeth to get at the sweet nuts inside. In October it was conkers we went for. There never seemed to be enough of these to keep the conker fights going.

The community of children amused and occupied itself in a multitude of ways. Most mothers and fathers were endlessly busy and not well-off enough to buy many toys, so there was plenty of opportunity for our improvisation and invention. We built tree houses and hedge houses, and constructed kites of all sizes which we flew in the back field. We made stilts to walk tall on, using binder string fixed to giant up-turned empty jam tins. The branches of alder trees were cut up and turned into pop-guns to battle with, firing shelled acorns. And then, in November, came our greatest co-operative venture – the building of a huge bonfire on the back field for Guy Fawkes Night.

Bird-nesting

Living at the edge of the village meant that as children we entered into the life of the fields at an early age. It was safe to roam alone along the hedges and ditches. Sometimes there would be two or three of us together. I do not remember feeling any danger in daylight, once I had reached the age of nine. Of course there were mushrooms it wasn't wise to touch, deadly nightshade berries not to be swallowed, ponds not to be fallen into. We were warned by our parents never to pick up sweets from the roadways – they might have been poisoned. Farmers didn't like us to run into the crops so we stuck to the hedgerows and hid in the ditches. In spring we hunted for birds' nests. The delight of finding four or five speckled-blue thrush's eggs warm in the nest was a high peak in experience – pure unalloyed delight. Birds had laid them. Young and innocent, I did not possess the knowledge of bird biology. 'Laid' was what the table was before meals. 'Lay out the plates, knives and forks', was what Mum asked me to do. I therefore had little idea of how or why the eggs were laid. They could have been plucked out of the air by the birds in flight, could have floated down from the clouds. The eggs might once have been pebbles in streams, turned by magic into eggs. My mother, after all, placed china eggs in the hens' nests to persuade them to start laying. If china eggs were turned into real eggs ... there must be a connection.

We boys, who usually bird-nested in pairs, only stole sample eggs. We calculated that the parent birds couldn't count, and so would not miss one or two. Freshly laid eggs were easy to blow. We had all that was necessary in the top lapels of our jackets – a thick sewing needle. Making a small hole at each end of the egg, we would then blow the contents on to the ground beneath. If the wind was blowing the stuff fell on to our shoes. It never occurred to me that there would be one thrush or blackbird the less as a result.

The Harvest Field

It was high summer that brought real joy into my heart. As the sun got warmer and the days got longer I knew that the nearby fields of corn, oats or barley would be ready to cut in the middle of August. All summer we boys had watched and waited. Then word would filter down from those in the know, the adults, that a certain field was ready. 'They're cutting tomorrow up the Wong Loke', was the message transmitted by word of mouth from adult to child. The signal for this activity was the scything of the entire edge of the field the day before. This was to give space for the horse-drawn binder to have a clear run. For the village boys the action we wanted was the chasing of rabbits, all hiding in the crop. Equipped with sticks or cudgels as we called them, we patrolled the field awaiting the first signs of movement in the corn – the trembling of a late poppy-head or the gentle waving of a few corn-stalks. If this happened we were expected to yell out phrases like 'Here's one!' or 'There's one!' or 'Get it!' 'Stand back!' 'It's coming!' 'Go on!' Our knotty ended sticks would be lifted to shoulder level ready for the chase. If there were men with dogs and guns we boys felt a bit cheated. We were made to stand back and 'let the dog see the rabbit' as the men said. Our chances of making a capture and taking home a dinner for the family faded in the noise of dogs yelping and guns firing. I hated the guns and feared the dogs. Although I shared the ambition of the others and the intense excitement generated, I never ever managed to catch a rabbit. I ran through the rough stubble with the rest, shouted, pointed, fell over sheaves, fell into horse droppings, waved my cudgel around but not once did I get near enough to strike a blow to the head of any one of those terrified, fleeing rabbits. In other fields I had seen boys parading about with a brace of furry little dead creatures, tied on to sticks across their shoulders. Perhaps, even then, I knew that I did not have what it took to kill anything. I couldn't manage a butterfly with a pin. If I accidentally cut a worm in half with my spade in the garden I felt bad about it, but consoled myself in the belief that each half would turn into another whole worm and the two of them would crawl off happily together.

Where this extreme 'reverence for life' attitude sprung from

I cannot easily discern. The other boys seemed quite at ease killing the fish they caught in streams, beating frogs and toads to pieces, crushing snails, flattening butterflies, and moths. Somehow I was too squeamish or frightened, or sensitive to join in the slaughter. Perhaps it all went back to the sense of wonder with which I had been introduced to the world of nature. 'Look at that!' Mum or Dad would say and one's eyes would be directed to some quite humble phenomenon of nature. 'Smell that!' would be the cry and one's nose would be shoved into a cascading blossom. 'Feel that!' 'Listen to this!' 'Watch here!' There was a continuous call to wonder. It has never quite left me. The old feeling always returns every time I see a dandelion clock – that amazing globe of tiny parachuting seeds. When I pick one up, blow the seeds gently to be scattered by the winds, I can cheat Time. One o'clock, two o'clock, three o'clock, ten o'clock, eleven o'clock, twelve o'clock – any time I like.

Later, by the real noon on the harvest field, much has already happened. The labourers have had their 'elevenses' – a bottle of cold tea, some sandwiches or pieces of pie. About half of the field is already cut. The sheaves are now standing in groups of six, leaning on each other. There are gaps underneath where we can creep in and hide. These little tunnels are like tiny houses to us – the straw smell, the thatched roof feel, just like a cottage home.

But now the first upset of the day arrives. The string mechanism on the binder has gone wrong. The string can no longer tie up the bundles of corn around their waists to turn them into sheaves. The stuff is just strewn round wherever it has landed from the whirling blades of the binder through the knife blades and from off the canvas belt. We shall have to sit around waiting for the repairs to be carried out. That will take a long time.

Conversations begin. 'Them ould hosses don't break down yu know, not like them bloody ould machines.' The man who said that had got the point. The poverty of the farming villages in the thirties meant that much of the farm machinery was second-hand or worn out. Most of my childhood was haunted by broken-down gadgets, rusty bicycles, toys that had seen their day, clocks and watches whose springs had broken. The ball bearings of my first second-hand bike were jammed after the first ride. An old gramophone somebody had given me had a problem with the governors which controlled the speed of the record. The dance of the cygnets from Swan Lake is quite unforgettable at 100 turns a minute.

Matching these personal difficulties for children with small things, were the farmers' problems with larger things. The falling-down barns, the broken field-gates, the overgrown hedgerows and uncleared ditches, the odd clapped-out car ferried to the gravel pit, and dumped.

In this experience of economic hardships I think I can detect the seeds of an attitude that has haunted me since. Thence came my absolute distrust of all machinery, my solid expectation that things are going to break up, wind down, go rusty, rot away and turn to dust. But 'them hosses' will never break down – they go on for ever.

It is now late afternoon on the harvest field. All looks neat and tidy. The sheaves are all stacked up in stooks but a quarter of the crop is still standing. Suddenly the binder stops. This time things have gone wrong with the cutting edges of the blade. Our worst fears are confirmed. We children are aware that if that small part of the field is left uncut overnight the rabbits and hares will escape into the darkness. From past observation we know that dozens of them are making a last frantic stand in there. For us boys the main purpose of the whole enterprise is lost.

As the horses are unharnessed from the broken binder we fear that we must wait for the next field or the one after that to once again renew the excitement of the hunt. Rabbit pie may still be on the menu, but only on the far horizon.

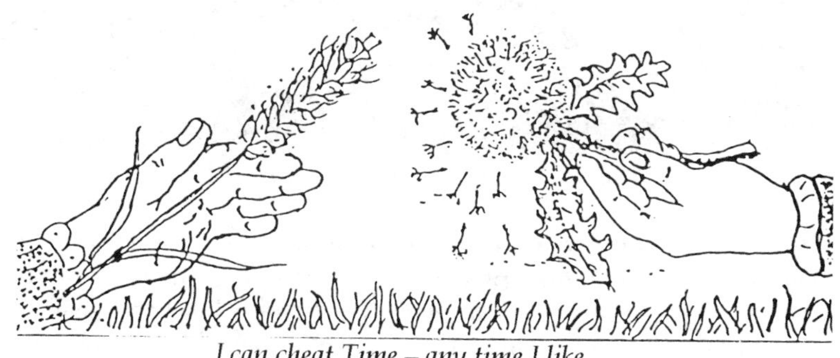

I can cheat Time – any time I like ...

SOME EARLIEST FEARS

Rock-a-bye baby

There was a wind which local people said blew straight across from Siberia to the plains of East Anglia. Some nights it certainly howled round the corner of the house where my bedroom was. One nursery rhyme stays with me most from early remembrances:

> Rock-a-bye baby on the tree-top,
> When the wind blows the cradle will rock,
> When the bough breaks the cradle will fall
> And down will come baby, cradle and all.

I don't remember ever being in a cradle, certainly not in a cradle on a treetop, so there was no echo of any traumatic experience.

When the bough breaks the cradle will fall ...

Perhaps this particular rhyme hung about in my memory because it suggested the precarious nature of life, the uncertainty and dangers of just existing in the world. 'Rock-a-bye baby' seemed to symbolise the general fear of falling, fear of falling into water, into mud, into snow. An atmosphere of anxiety and apprehension surrounded my early childhood. This I think sprang from my mother. Her fears were no doubt of falling into hard times and poverty. Most of the other nursery rhymes had little impact on my consciousness, but 'Rock-a-bye baby' was the one that held a hidden message just for me.

A Terrible Old Hole

A misunderstanding of some words my mother used when I was about four years old served to reinforce the feelings of dread which sometimes clouded my otherwise happy childhood. We had just moved into a little farm cottage, a tied cottage. It was Michaelmas time – October, that is. My father was to be employed for the following year until the end of harvest. The cottage had not been left very clean by the previous tenants. My mother was scrubbing out the place. I can see her now, down on her knees in the kitchen. She has a scrubbing brush in her hand and a bucket of hot water by her side. It is a red-brick floor. As she scrubs she says, 'This is a terrible old hole, this is a terrible old hole.' Of course she probably meant the whole house, or even the whole hamlet, which, incidentally, was appropriately called Griselwood. But for me, with my habit of taking words too literally, it meant that there in the kitchen, beneath the red bricks, was a 'terrible old hole', like a well. And into this hole would fall rock-a-bye baby boy, out of his cradle, off the bough, and down into something terrible.

Sally Wiseman

Sally Wiseman had a little sweetshop. It was a small part of the front of her house, just a few doors away from where we lived when I was about five years old. Sally was a quiet, gentle old lady. To buy sweets we went through the front door, which sounded a bell. Sally would appear behind the tall counter. My usual request was for a halfpenny bag of sweets or sometimes even a farthing bag. We got quite a lot of sweets for that money in those days – humbugs, sherbet dips, sweethearts and liquorice sticks. Some older boys told me that if I spent sixpence I could get a bag of sweets that would change me from a boy into a girl. Why I believed this I can't imagine. There was little chance of me ever having sixpence to buy the miraculous bag of sweets. But the frightening thing was just the idea that such a change could occur. I was, after all, mother's blue-eyed rock-a-bye boy and I was quite happy in my boyhood.

Chicken Licken

Another tormenting fear of early childhood was once again connected with my misunderstanding of words, and the muddling up of fact and fiction.

The flatness of the countryside made for a lot of sky and

masses of clouds to fill it all. The journey home from the village school to my house led in a westerly direction. The sun was unusually low in the sky late in the afternoons of winter. I used to trot home with all that sky hanging over my head. One particular afternoon – I must have been six or seven years old – my head was full of a story I had been reading in my school primer. It concerned one Chicken Licken, upon whose little head an acorn had fallen from the sky. The falling of this acorn led Chicken Licken to alert his friends, Turkey Lurky, Henny Penny and Ducky Lucky, together with the rest of a group of farmyard creatures with similarly strange double-barrelled names, and to tell them of the danger that the sky was about to fall. They must go to see the King and report this event. For me, Chicken Licken was as real as the chickens my mother kept in our back garden. The acorn was as real as the acorns which, at that time of the year, were falling from the giant oak trees by the road side. The King was real – his picture, after all, was on the postage stamps I saw.

This must mean, therefore, that there was a danger that the sky above me would fall. There was so much sky and it looked very heavy to me. Nothing seemed to be holding it up. There were no sky-hooks. Clouds moved menacingly, colours changed and the wind blew. I became Chicken Licken. I ran like the wind to get home to Mum before the sky could fall, and do whatever skies do when they fall on rock-a-bye boys and Chicken Lickens on winter afternoons.

The Snow Queen

Other stories were equally frightening for me. I had too much identification with the characters, in this case with the boy Kay and his friend Gerda. It is the part of the fairy story where the sky has been filled with tiny fragments of ice, like almost invisible pieces of glass. Perhaps a mirror in the sky has been broken. Kay and Gerda are looking out of their window. Some of the icy fragments fall into Kay's eyes. These snow-cold pieces go down into his heart. Little Kay then changes from being a loving, sweet boy to a cold-hearted, hating boy – a boy who no longer loves his friend Gerda. His heart has turned to ice. Could this fate befall me if I looked out through the open window when snow or hail were falling? Would I then start to be cold to my sister Irene? Rock-a-bye boys must not be left out on the treetop in the falling snow. Chicken Licken must not be caught in a farmyard blizzard. The menace from the sky hung over the land of living children.

The Fender
Fear of the consequences of unemployment was never far from the poorer members of the village community, Mum and Dad included. One day, during my seventh year, I walked home from school to our tiny cottage, for the midday meal, to find my mother down on her hands and knees in front of the fireplace. She was using blacking polish to shine the smallish movable cast-iron fender.

As I bent down to kiss her cheek I was surprised to see tears falling down her face. She began to sob.

'What's the matter, Mum?' I asked.

'Your Dad's lost his job and I don't know how we are going to make ends meet.' She was still polishing the black fender. I gazed at the fender. How would we be able to make ends meet? I wondered about that, sensing the desperate nature of the situation. Dad was to lose his job as milk-roundsman at the Thickthorn Hall Farm. Of course I lacked the understanding of such phrases as 'making ends meet'. It had to be something to do with that fender. If only, I thought, if only the two ends of that black fender could be bent round so that they would meet, then everything would be all right and my poor mother could stop crying. I longed to do the metal bending myself. There was no thought in my little mind about the consequences of changing the shape of the fender. My geometry was unconcerned about making the fender useless for its real purpose of keeping the embers from setting light to the rag-rug by the fire. No! Life had presented me with a first exercise in imaginative problem-solving, to stop my mother from crying, to find my father another job, to have the fire blazing again in the empty grate. All of these things did indeed come about – but of course it was none of my doing.

Bridges
I suffered much fear about bridges. There was a rather narrow stone-walled bridge over the River Yare at Cringleford, a village on the way to Norwich, our nearest city. My fear of crossing bridges dated back to the fact that my father told me how a heavy steam engine had been crossing that bridge one day when something went badly wrong. The engine crashed through the wall and fell into the river far below, and the driver was killed. Cringleford bridge was a bit 'hump backed'. If a bus went across rather fast all of us passengers would be lifted up and dropped back into our seats. Most children

enjoyed the feeling they got in the pit of the stomach – like being on a swing in mid-air. But for me there was a perpetual terror which seized me every time we approached that bridge – perhaps once a fortnight, on a market day. I would sit hoping and praying that the bus would get safely over. If we could just get across and only then the bridge could collapse, just a few feet only would do, and I would be happy again. Unfortunately, this fear spread to all the bridges in my known world: Bawburgh bridge, Marlingford bridge and, worst of all, Acle bridge, which was made of wood. Who could be mad enough to make a bridge from boughs of trees, I thought? The noise made by the rattling of the wooden planks, as vehicles crossed that bridge added to my fright. We had to go over Acle bridge once a year when we travelled in charabancs on Sunday School outings to the seaside at Yarmouth. The outing was the high point of the summer. I foresaw that all our six charabancs, full of children and their parents, were all to weigh down on Acle bridge. The thought terrified me. I would scheme in my mind whether it was safer to be in the leading bus or in the last one. As the bus I was sitting in approached the dreaded bridge I breathed out, stood up to reduce the weight on the seat, prayed, hoped and kept my fingers crossed. I daren't even hope that the bridge would go down just after my bus got over, for the others behind us would hurtle into the river. I visualised the whole scene in terror. The bridge fear, I believe, lasted from my sixth to my ninth year but as far as I know no bridges fell during that time – just the ones in my head, which fell over and over again.

Against the Darkness

I do not remember one streetlight in the village during my childhood. I have memories of unending darkness stretching far over the land and filling the sky. As a boy I was frightened on nights when I walked home alone to our house at the edge of the village. The road was a lonely one. I never knew whether to run or walk. I felt sure somebody was lurking in the hedge to grab me from behind and carry me off. My way of dealing with this fear was to hold my torch facing backwards into the darkness behind while walking forwards into the darkness in front. This must have worked because, happily, I always reached home safely. The outer darkness was one thing, the inside darkness another. As I climbed the dark stairs to my unlit room I feared that someone would be hiding under the bed. So each night I lifted the hanging down bedcover, shone my torch around under the bed just to see. Of course, there was never anyone there. I am not sure what I would have done if I had found somebody.

The darkness everywhere in the village caused much confusion. Without a torch it was easy to become lost – to end up in the wrong house or the wrong garden. A Methodist local preacher I knew in my childhood, a sweet, sincere but rather dreamy man, preached on Sundays in outlying village chapels. It was not a paid job. There were few country buses on Sundays so he walked if the distance was short, but for longer journeys he took his bicycle. One Sunday he went from Norwich to East Tuddenham, a journey of about twelve miles. He spent the day there, taking the morning and evening services. After that he started out for home on his bicycle. The road was long, straight, and flat, with trees and hedges on both sides. It was a rough night of wind and rain. When he was about halfway home a heavy gust blew out his front light. Unable to relight it while facing the wind, he turned his bicycle right round so that the oil lamp was sheltered. He struck his matches and relit the lamp, but forgot to turn his bicycle round. He mounted again and rode on into the darkness. Three-quarters of an hour later he arrived back at the village he had started from, where he had preached his two sermons. Some weeks later, with much humour, he related the adventure to us – a story against himself, against a too straight road and against the darkness.

It was not uncommon, even for people who knew our village well, to sometimes lose their way on dark nights. My father was a member of the village brass band. Brass bands and male voice choirs abounded in the villages at that time. The band had about 20 members in its hey day. Dad loved being in it. At Christmas time one year some of the keener members went round the village at night playing carols outside big houses and small houses to raise money for the band. Sometimes they were invited in for mince pies or sausage rolls, and a glass of Stone's Green Ginger Wine. At each stop they played three or four carols before sending someone with a collecting box to knock on the door. The only light they had was from an oil lantern held aloft on a shepherd's crook. Some of the houses were set well back from the road or behind huge hedges in back lanes. Towards the end of their journey they were ready for a last call. Perhaps the ginger wine had made them less observant of local geography. They played the four carols merrily outside a house hardly visible in the dark. They waited while the man with the box went off to collect. After a while he returned laughing: 'We've made a big mistake here together, we've bin a-playing to a bloomin' haystack.' No money, no mince pies, no Stone's Ginger. Later the bandsmen laughingly told their story. As they rightly said, haystacks were just like houses in the dark!

Still, there were times when we blessed the darkness of the countryside. There were compensations. The darker the night, the brighter the stars. Starlit nights were a delight for me as a child. My parents pointed out the Plough, the Bear and the Milky Way. My neck ached from looking up at these distant visions. Just hunting for them, just finding them, naming them, was joy enough. A whole sky full of stars with only us gazing up. It was odd and awe-inspiring.

BEING USEFUL

The Duck-pluckers' Dinner

The first activity which could conceivably be called a job involving a wage and conditions of employment was a joint venture with my sister, Irene. She would be about eight and I would be about six. Our mother did cleaning and washing for a Mrs Neave, who had a much larger house than ours just over the road from us. Mrs Neave took in lodgers. Two of these lodgers were duck-pluckers who worked in a building which was not far from the village school. For the sum of threepence a week my sister and I were to transport the midday meal for these two men, by foot and basket, one hand on each side of the wicker basket, and our feet walking in step so as not to disturb the contents. It was always a hot meal cooked by Mrs Neave, well covered to keep it warm on the journey. The walk was about half a mile. Irene and I would come home from school for our lunch, and then pick up the lodgers' basket from Mrs Neave. This simple and effective plan we could manage easily.

I found the duck-pluckers' establishment a place quite beyond belief. The air was full of feathers and fine dust of a feathery nature. There was a strange, powerful duck smell. In one section there were freshly delivered wooden crates containing live ducks quacking and squawking in chorus. Hanging from the dark beams of the low building were ducks ready for plucking. Somewhere in the dark rear of this barn-like place, duck killing must have been carried out, although my sister and I never witnessed that. The men sat on a wooden bench, side by side. They worked at incredible speed, holding the ducks between their knees and rapidly pulling the feathers off. As the feathers flew and fell to the ground, the white flesh of the ducks appeared, all ready for market.

We were always given a friendly welcome by the two men, Bob and Harold. They had probably been working since eight in the morning and were consequently ready for their food when we arrived. Having delivered it, Irene and I would go on to the school playground to await the afternoon session.

This job of dinner delivery went smoothly for many weeks. But then something went disastrously wrong. No, we didn't drop the basket and spill everything. What really happened was so bad that I must have blotted out some of it from my memory. It seems that one day my sister, at some point on the journey, had lifted the protective cloth in the basket, then lifted the lid of the basin containing the steak and kidney pudding, and had put her fingers through the pastry and helped herself to a few fingers full. Tell-tale signs of her invasion must have been left. I don't remember whether I took part in the operation. But I do remember the child court martial which mother conducted later. Her face showed her disappointment. 'I'm really vexed!' she said. Mother always said that when we'd fallen from grace. 'I'm really vexed!'

Needless to say the upshot was that we lost the contract, together with the weekly payment which had supplemented our pocket money. From that experience I think that I learned three important lessons for later life: goods in transit are a sacred trust; light-fingered pudding stealers are bound to be found out; it is risky to go into partnership.

The white flesh of the ducks appeared ...

Pig Scraping

My mother did a cleaning job for Mrs Smith, the butcher's wife. I would be between six and seven years old at that time, and always went with her. I used to take my clay pipe to blow bubbles while I waited. Mother would mix up the soapy water and give me a jam jar with enough to make hundreds of bubbles. I also had my matchbox with cotton-wool-and-matchstick people in it. I usually sat under the appletree on the lawn, playing while my mother slaved away at cleaning and polishing Mrs Smith's house. As I grew a little older, Mr Smith the butcher thought to involve me in simple tasks of his trade. I was allowed to turn the handle of the large mincing machine, which fed the sausage meat into the yards of skin to make the sausages. From that I moved on to turning the handle of the heavy grindstone on which the butcher sharpened his knives. Both these jobs I performed with some zeal. But the day came when one of the pigs had to be killed. I was made to stay out of the way at the front of the house, keeping well away from the outhouses round the back. I sensed that something terrible was about to happen. The air was filled with the squealing of the pig as the knife, which I had helped to sharpen, cut its throat. Later in the day, I was given a metal scraper. The pig's body was in a large, round, wooden tub in quite hot water. The steam came up into my face. My job was to help scrape the bristles off the white skin so that the butcher would have clean joints of pork to sell in his shop. To this day I can recapture and re-create the smell of the bristles of the not-long-dead pig. The knife which I had helped to sharpen became the feared symbol of a sudden death. All my life since then I have kept well away from grindstones, sharp knives and pigs.

Toy Boxes

In 1930, when I was eight years old, a most important event happened which changed the life of our family. Up till then we had lived in a variety of broken-down tied cottages which went with Dad's job as a farm labourer. But, on the outskirts of many Norfolk villages, council houses were being built for renting to poorer families. We were lucky enough to be offered one of these. Our house was in a row of twelve on the edge of Hethersett, overlooking fields, woods and a distant glen. Mother called it 'Glen-view'. We were all tremendously excited. Great plans were made for the garden and the house itself. For the first time we had electricity instead of Primus stoves, paraffin lamps and candles.

Our father made us two wooden boxes just about twelve inches square, with hinged lids. The boxes were covered with brown Rexine. The lids were padded for us to be able to sit one on each side of the coal fire in the living room. Under the four corners of the boxes, at the bases, were 'domes of silence' so that the boxes could be slid about on the floor without damaging the lino. Domes of silence may now be called castors. I much prefer the earlier name. These boxes were to be our toy boxes. Every Friday afternoon, mother would give the order, 'All right then, tidy out your toy boxes.' By the glow and warmth of the fire we would carry out this task. One square foot is a puzzle for organising the storage of an assortment of anything at all, let alone toys. There were no side shelves or compartments. It resembled the problem of modern top-loading freezers. The whole operation took an hour or two. We discarded surplus stock, especially after Christmas. Mother would then come in from the kitchen, and pronounce her satisfaction or otherwise. I think we enjoyed the task; I certainly did. From that experience I learned an important lesson that has since stood me in good stead. It taught me to love cleaning out and tidying places, reordering the contents to improve things. I learned how to fit large amounts of objects into seemingly inadequate spaces, also to remember just where items have been hidden so as to make instant retrieval possible. My delight in such activities has been life-long.

As a grown-up, the biggest task of this nature I undertook for friends was to clear out and reorganise an old barn they had inherited. It was like a giant toy box. The operation took two days and gave me enormous pleasure. My friends said they could never have managed it. They had not been toy box trained.

When I left home as a young man my toybox came with me. For years it served some useful purpose. But wear and tear perhaps destined it to a fire in some garden or it may have been left behind in a loft at house-moving time. Yet the image of that toy box is imprinted at the back of my mind so that whenever I find sheds, cupboards, rooms, suitcases, trunks that need filling or emptying, the old delight returns. My life has been box-filled. I love them all – shoe boxes, card-index boxes, orange boxes and the strong cardboard boxes that wine bottles are delivered in.

When my wife and I recently moved house I collected 250 such empty boxes from various wine merchants. I packed them full of books, gramophone records, crockery, cutlery and other such adult toys. They were just the right weight and size for carrying around the house to the removal van, and so on. I should like to depart this life, when my time comes, in a well-made wooden box, covered, if possible, with shiny brown Rexine and with a hinged lid for making my escape.

Potato Harvest

Potato cultivation was one of the main uses of our new, long back garden. By the time I was nine I had almost mastered the art of digging. My father had taught me how to dig and we took pleasure in watching the rich black undersoil come off the shiny spades. Each row we dug was an achievement to be noted. We counted out the rows and measured the fresh black earth. A day or two later after we had raked the surface of the earth he would stretch a rope across the garden. He then made holes of the right size and depth with a wooden dibble. I moved along and planted a seed potato in each hole. The holes were then covered over. During the next few months all the usual things that needed to be done were done to the rows of ripening potato plants. Then, at the right time, Dad would test a root. He always knew when the crop was ready. Now was the signal for our potato harvest to begin and the forks would come out of the shed. I had to learn to keep my fork well back from the root so as not to spear any potato. Spearing was the worst thing you could do to a new potato. Each root that we lifted up was inspected for size and number. There was a playful rivalry between Dad and myself to see who could get the biggest haul.

'Here's a whopper!' he'd call.

'Here's a whopper!' I'd call in answer.

Some of the larger potatoes, the giants, would have already broken the thin stems joining them to the root. These were still hidden in the soil and had to be prized out by hand and not by fork. Others were still joined to the stems and needed to be shaken off. Some of these little ones we described as 'babies'. The tiniest were thrown away, maybe over the neighbour's hedge. The smell of the earth, the leaves, the roots and the smell of the potatoes themselves filled my nostrils. I loved it. The odd robin flew over to catch worms from the newly dug soil where we placed each potato to dry in the sun and wind. One day as we were working I must have spotted amongst all these new potatoes something which looked like a diseased one. Dad said, 'Tha's a badun.' The skin was all wrinkled and flabby. The inside was soft and jelly-like to the touch. This potato was clearly decomposing. 'Tha's the mother potato, throw it away!' said Dad. The word 'mother' surprised me. What terrible truth might lie behind that word? I then saw it all in a flash. The fine firm potato which I had planted in the spring had completed its life's task and was now ready for the scrap-heap, ready to join the rubbish where potato peelings, apple cores, lemon peel, orange peel, egg-shells, burnt toast, and burnt porridge all ended. I thought of my paternal grandmother and the fourteen children she had produced, one of whom was my own father. I thought of my mother and the two children she had produced, one of whom was myself. Was this the way the world went? The answer was there lying in the soil at the end of an old garden fork.

I thought of my grandmother and the fourteen children she had produced …

Leaf-mould

I discovered quite early in life the concept of piece-work – where the worker is paid, not by the hour, but by the amount of production. This was illustrated for me by one of the first jobs my father gave my sister Irene and me when we moved into the new house. The soil of the new garden had much clay in it. After all, the place had been just a field before. There was a desperate need for leaf-soil. The autumn trees produced the leaves in abundance. They were all lying by the side of the roads that led down to the Running Stream, our favourite playing place. Dad offered us a halfpenny for each sack of leaves we would collect. That was the rate for the job – real piece-work. All we needed was our four-wheeled go-kart, a broom and two thin pieces of plywood for picking up the heaps of leaves, and six bags to stuff the leaves into. We worked with a will, dragging our cart up the hill from the Running Stream back to the house where we unloaded the sacks and counted them carefully. The thing about piece-work was that it seemed like carrots to a donkey. You saw the halfpennies mounting up. Grown men are heard to talk about 'killing the job' which means working too fast. This, they would say, brings the price down next time. We had no such knowledge or considerations. I seem to remember that we persuaded the next-door children to help us, to bring their go-kart, broom and bags. It was a case of over-production, another way of killing the job. We made such a huge heap of leaves in the back garden that Dad had to call us off. That week our pocket money was much enhanced. The roadsides on the way to the Running Stream were cleaner of leaves than they had ever been. The eventual outcome was when these myriad leaves were buried in the soil at digging time, and allowed to rot, becoming the rich brown leaf-mould which greatly helped the growing of flowers and vegetables alike.

Acorns and Horse Muck

About a year later, Bob Richardson, a young local farmer, and friend of the family, offered Irene and me another piece-work job. He kept pigs on his father's farm. According to him, pigs loved to eat acorns. There were many oak trees round the meadows which he farmed by the Running Stream. Bob offered to pay us sixpence a bushel of collected acorns. Until then I had only a vague idea about bushels. I had heard that you were not supposed to hide your light under one and on the back of our blue, shiny, school writing books, amongst the lists of tables there were items about yards, chains, furlongs, together with items about gills, pints and gallons, rods, poles, and perches. I knew that a perch was a fish and that fishes had gills. Rods were for beating naughty children, and poles were for flags or telegraph wires. It was all very confusing. There was also mention of pecks and bushels. But to meet a real bushel in a real field of acorns was to meet real mathematics. Filling the bushel baskets which Bob the farmer had provided took many hours. It was back-bending, back-aching work. During the collecting I thought of the pigs knocking back a breakfast of these tough-skinned shiny fruit of the great oak trees. I had once eaten an acorn while picking blackberries on a hedgerow and I was terribly sick within an hour. Altogether we collected just six bushels. By the time that was finished I knew the shape of an acorn, an acorn-cup and a dead oak leaf. I knew their textures and colours. Their shapes entered the repertoire of things I could draw easily from memory.

Following hard on the heels of acorn-gathering came more piece-work, this time from Dad. In those days there were few cars on the roads of the village. Quite a lot of horse-drawn carts and horse-drawn machinery passed along the highway by our house. The milk-cart and pony came past twice a day. Mum and Dad needed even richer soil for the garden to go along with the leaf-mould. I was equipped with a small metal pail and a small black coal shovel. What the price per bucket was I don't quite remember but whenever a horse was heard trotting or galloping by I would be alerted to get out there quickly in case any of the neighbours' children had the same idea. I have never found anything unpleasant about horse muck. The steam that arose around a freshly landed heap of horse manure always had a straw smell about it, which I liked, but I always wondered whether horses really enjoyed eating all that straw. I pictured them breaking it up with their huge teeth. This picture was preferable to the one I had of pigs grinding acorns to pulp and grunting their way through one bushel after another.

Being More Useful

Piece-work, however, was not the golden rule. For much of our childhood our duty was to help with household jobs and there were tasks which we performed regularly. Everything from collecting hogweed for the rabbits and cleaning out their hutches, to cleaning and polishing the spoons, knives, and forks. I must have held miles of skeins of wool for my mother and sister in turn while they wound it into balls for knitting. I shelled peas and broad beans, peeled potatoes in winter, and scraped them in summer. There was joy in some of this labour, especially if our efforts were praised. My sister and I knew all about work before we reached the age of ten.

One of my usual jobs was to chop the sticks for lighting our coal fires. Coal scuttles full of rich, black pieces of coal had to be brought into the house. Chopping the sticks was a Saturday morning job. The wood was rough, pine, box-wood. It usually split easily when hit with a metal chopper. The sticks were not to be too thick or too thin. Variety came when there was a knot in the wood. Then the chopper jumped about and sometimes hit the concrete floor of the shed where I worked on my haunches or kneeling down. Then the sparks flew or I might even hurt my finger, go to Mum, and have a bandage put on. Apart from this, the job required no concentration so thoughts could wander or the mind could stay empty – both were valued alternatives.

My second regular task was cleaning the family's shoes. This was also a Saturday morning job. Here more care and attention was called for. If the weather had been bad that week then the mud had to be scraped off the bottoms and sides of the shoes. A major crime was polishing over dried mud. The brushes must not be muddled up, nor the tins of Cherry Blossom polish mixed up. If I polished brown shoes with black brushes my sins would find me out. All the family also expected a high shine on their shoes even if the shoes were past their best. As I worked away I can remember puzzling over the Cherry Blossom shoe polish advertisement on the covers of the tins. What had these two shiny cherries to do with boot polish? For me cherry blossom referred to the flowers only and not to the fruit. I was also puzzled by the advertisement for Robin Starch and couldn't see any connection with the little robin redbreasts which hopped and flew about the garden. As an adult I still object to the theft of words like 'tide' and 'surf' to name soap powders and words like 'mushroom cloud' upset me, and names of pop groups such as 'Marmalade', and 'Tyrannosaurus Rex' confuse me. How strange I think it is to have newspapers called *The Sun*, *Evening Star* and *Morning Star*. I feel that the language is somehow betrayed.

When I reached the age of ten I was strong enough to fetch pails of water from the pump at the front of the garden, near the gate. Though this was heavy work there was pleasure too. The contact with the elemental stuff of the world – fire, earth and water – always had a special fascination. I never really understood how the pump worked. Just to lift the handle up and down, and wait for the water to shoot out seemed far too easy a way to produce such gushings of pure, cold water. Fetching the pails into the house without spillage was clearly an important job. I felt that the whole household depended on me to bring it in. Everything from tea-making, cooking, washing up dinner things, washing clothes and the weekly baths in the metal bungalow-bath all relied on a good supply of water. So I pumped and fetched, and carried with a will.

MEETING GOD

My dear, good parents got themselves converted in their late twenties when I was seven years old. Getting converted, as it was called, was an intense experience with many repercussions for them and for the rest of the family. They got converted from not being religious at all to being very religious indeed. Grandma Symonds told us many years later that joining the chapel had changed my parents a great deal. From being happy and laughing they had become serious, and rather heavy-laden. She thought it was not a good thing at all.

The conversions happened at the Hethersett Methodist Chapel in the village to which we had recently moved. The effects filtered down to me, and powerfully influenced the subsequent years of my childhood and adolescence.

Until that time I had been aware of, and in awe of, certain big things in my little world. I had seen a big train. Then there were huge, tall trees growing all over the place. Only the sun was small to look at, as was the moon. Stars were very small indeed. The clouds could be quite big and I could see their edges. The sky itself was very big but did not have edges to mark out its bigness. And so meeting God was a puzzling experience of quite a different order. I think the first encounter was on the way home from Sunday School one afternoon. There must have been some talk in the lesson of God seeing all. As I walked home I considered the matter. To see all of us on the ground I thought God must have an eye. To see all of us the eye would have to be very big. That is how I saw it. Literally up there in the sky. A huge eye bigger than a cloud, hovering half-way between the chapel and Kenny Wood's Loke near my home. My God had only one eye. I surmised that the only time the eye could not see what we were up to was when dark clouds blocked the view. I cannot remember whether the vision frightened me or whether it made me feel more important to be thus observed. The great eye was there for me for a few years. Hanging in the sky it looked down on Randall's field of cabbages, on Yull's ruined cottage and on the cornfields opposite our house, and on me.

Inside our home, at that time, on the living-room wall opposite where I sat at meal-times, there was an inscription on a piece of plywood. The wood was framed with gold and the lettering was embossed and in manuscript style. The text announced with a certain authority:

Christ is the head of this house
The Unseen Guest at every meal
The Unseen Listener to every conversation

and more of the same which I cannot now remember. I took this seriously. I suppose that Mum and Dad did as well.

The idea of this presence in the house was less menacing than the big eye outside. This unseen guest was on the human scale because our chairs, plates, knives and forks were only suitable for humans. This listener to conversations must have normal-sized ears. The idea was altogether more manageable. The presence could walk up and down the stairs, and round the rooms easily.

I seem to remember an empty chair was placed at one end of the table for a few meal-times. A shortage of chairs a little later led to the provision only of an empty plate. After a time the symbolic ritual was dropped altogether. My tendency to believe all that I read or was told at chapel made my life bewildering. I did not question the right of this holy lodger to float around the house. But I learned to look for an escape. There must be some way out from the presence of Jesus. I worked out that the unseen guest did not inhabit our outdoor lavatory. It was far too cold and smelt too strongly of Jeyes Fluid. The torn up pieces of newspaper hanging on a string from the wall would not make good reading for any guest. In the outdoor lavatory one was therefore free to think primitive thoughts, talk to oneself without being overheard. There were primitive realities to be faced, the animal nature to be attended to. My longing for privacy made this cold, whitewashed shed a sacred retreat.

Meanwhile my parents threw themselves wholeheartedly into all the activities of the chapel. Their enthusiasm for all things holy and evangelical knew no bounds. My sister and I were at services three or four times every Sunday, save for illness. Two or three times a week we attended various associated activities. This regime was kept up well into our teens. Sermons lasted from twenty minutes to three-quarters of an hour. Over the years, I must have listened to hundreds of them. Each week a different preacher came. I closed my eyes to countless prayers. I opened my mouth to sing innumerable hymns.

Hanging in the sky it looked down on Randall's field of cabbages ...

The building was simple. Nothing to detract from the religious meditation. There was little stained glass to speak of, no pictures, no crosses, but usually flowers in a prominent position. There were a few brass plates to commemorate the chapel founders. There was a huge clock which ticked away noisily near where we sat.

Perhaps this was to remind preachers not to go on for too long. The pews were simple – made of pine and varnished in a dark brown colour. The wood creaked as heavy worshippers stood up and sat down. In hot summers the varnish became sticky. Bits of me stuck to the seat. I remember the wrenching feeling at the back of my legs as I stood up at the end of a sermon. High up, the windows were of green glass and kept out a view of the sky. Windows at the back were home to hundreds of flies that swirled around endlessly. On summer Sundays their droning accompanied the sermons.

The hymn board hung by the preacher's head at the far end of the chapel. The hymns were the main focus of my thoughts about the nature and mystery of the Christian life. They were the main source of confusion, misunderstanding and bewilderment, but because the tunes were so beautiful the impact of the words went right into my heart. They still have the power to resonate.

Hymns

On most Sundays, after the preacher had chosen the hymns, my father brought the hymn board out of the vestry into the chapel and, climbing up the pulpit stairs, he would hang the board on the wall. Meanwhile the organist played a solemn piece of music while the congregation waited for the preacher to come in. Because I was aware of my parents' close involvement in the chapel services, I sensed that this worship was important and therefore must be taken seriously. And so I did. However, my childish propensity for always taking meaning in a literal sense, once again presented me, in the hymn singing, with many surrealist manifestations of the written word.

I do not quite know what John Keble meant when he wrote these words in the nineteenth century:

> There is a book who runs may read
> Which heavenly truth imparts.

The meaning was a challenge to my childish imagination. 'There is a book who runs may read.' Well, this book who runs must then have legs – either two legs or four legs. I preferred the two-legged variety, though the idea was uncanny. So I visualised the book on a huge scale not unlike the giant bibles found in church pulpits. The book who runs could travel along a country road. I saw it moving magically and swiftly, its great pages turning slowly in mid-air. Whoever wanted to read was running hard to keep up. If children today still sing it they might be forgiven for calling it a Jogger's Bible. My difficulties with the first two lines of the hymn prevented me from taking much interest in what followed as I cannot recall any of it. But apparently it was not the book which ran. The heavenly truths ran through the book and no doubt are still running.

Hymn number 158 in the *Methodist School Hymn Book* provided a further puzzle:

There is a green hill far away,
Without a city wall,
Where the dear Lord was crucified,
Who died to save us all.

For me the word 'without' signified a lack of something – coming indoors without wiping your shoes, going to bed without supper, coming downstairs without your socks on. So why was this green hill far away without a city wall round it? City walls were for protecting citizens. Norwich had a city wall, though it had fallen down in places. If only, I thought, that far away green hill had had a city wall round it perhaps the dear Lord would not have been crucified. Sadness for the green hill merged with sadness for the Lord.

Much of my time in chapel was spent in linguistic confusion and in trying to grasp concepts I was too young to deal with. But, amongst it all, certain things did become clear. In combining the messages from the hymns I recognised that something was expected of me. Jesus wanted me for a whole range of purposes.

Jesus wants me for a sunbeam
To shine for him each day . . .

I was prepared to be a sunbeam for him. After all, outside chapel we played at being all manner of thing. We became cars or aeroplanes; 'I'm a tea-pot, pour me out!' we said, doing the appropriate actions. But I understood that Jesus was for real. It was not acting.

Jesus bids us shine with a pure, clear light
Like a little candle burning in the night.

Yes, I knew about candles. They blew out in the wind. They set light to curtains. They stood in the windows of mothers whose sons had left home long ago but would one day return. Well, yes, I'd try to be a candle. But there was one hymn in which I was required to become something different in each of its five verses.

God make my life a little light
A little flame that burneth bright.

God make my life a little flower
That giveth joy to all.

God make my life a little staff
Whereon the weak may rest.

and lastly

God make my life a little hymn
Of tenderness and praise.

'A little hymn': I would read them, sing them, but how could I ever be one? There were further requirements: to be a pilgrim; to be a soldier; to be a knight in armour and to fight the good fight with all my might. It was a demanding schedule.

Other hymns revealed further mysteries. It transpired that Jesus was everywhere, not just an unseen guest in our house. Hymn number 129 said:

In our fertile cornfields
While the sheaves are bound,
In our busy markets
Jesus may be found.

So Jesus was out there with the rabbit catchers in Bob's field, and in the Norwich market-place by the fish and chip stall. I remember half longing, half dreading to meet him. There was an idea that I might see him walking on the sea at Yarmouth. But it was the Sankey and Moody hymn book, called *Sacred Songs and Solos,* with its 1,200 pieces, which put the real chill into my young spirits. Overpowering and frightening images rose up from its pages:

Rock of Ages cleft for me,
Let me hide myself in Thee;
Let the water and the blood
From thy riven side which flowed,
Be of sin the double cure.

In day school we had listened to the poem *The Pied Piper of Hamelin*. I had a clear picture in my mind of the mountain that opened up to let all the children follow the Piper out of the world to be lost for ever. So, for me, the rock of ages, as I imagined it, had the vast proportions of that mountain. The cleft was like a ravine. It was a dark place. Inside the rock nobody wore clothes. The water was on one side and the blood was on the other, like holy swimming-pools.

I think my vision of the swimming-pools came from another Sankey and Moody hymn:

There is a fountain filled with blood
Drawn from Immanuel's veins
And sinners plunged beneath that flood
Lose all their guilty stains.

The blood and water, with the notion of plunging in, provided my fearful swimming image. Here began my encounter with sin, guilt and redemption. It was a close and disturbing encounter, the repercussions of which experience stayed with me for a very long time.

Many hymns featured the after-life.

Where will you spend eternity?
The question comes to you and me.

That 'me' meant me. I gathered that eternity was reached at the end of life. Life was a tempestuous sea, the waters were dangerous, 'would your anchor hold' in the storms? There were rivers to be crossed and a far shore to be reached. Sankey and Moody number 1000 goes like this:

Shall we gather at the river
Where bright angel-feet have trod?
Yes, we'll gather at the river
The beautiful, the beautiful river,

Gather with the saints at the river
That flows by the throne of God.

At the age of seven I already had a vague idea about death. One day a horse-drawn carriage, which was carrying a coffin, taking a villager off to the churchyard, passed slowly by our cottage. This was my first awareness that humans actually died. In the years that followed our family made endless visits to churchyards and cemeteries. I learned to read tombstone inscriptions and learnt, incidentally, some arithmetic by working out how long someone had lived, and some Latin by reading words carved on the headstones. Whenever we visited villages we went to the churchyards. There was often little else of interest to see. The question often hovered at the back of my mind: 'Where will you spend eternity?' I was unable to work out if the newly buried dead were still under the grass, under the gravestones or already by the beautiful shore.

But amongst the gloomy hymns there were cheerful ones. At the end of harvest the chapel was filled with gifts from the farmers and gardeners. Every window sill was piled up with vegetables, fruit and crops of all kinds. There were loaves of bread in the shape of sheaves and a real sheaf of corn stood on the simple altar. The chapel was full of people and we sang triumphantly:

We plough the fields and scatter
The good seed on the land,
But it is fed and watered
By God's almighty hand.

There it was at last, the almighty hand. The almighty eye had been met with before. Meeting God in bits, even in large bits, added a surrealist dimension to my over-active imagination. God was nothing if not big.

There it was at last, the almighty hand;
God was nothing if not big…

WHAT FATHER DID

What Father Told Us

I often wonder what effect my father's accounts of his own childhood had on me in my own early days. Were those accounts a background against which I could map out my place in society? Did they help to stamp the marks of my social class upon me? In retrospect I am sure that they did those things. Assimilating my father's childhood experiences and family history contributed to my grounding in the world, to my feelings about the harsh realities of life and how these might be surmounted.

At the end of the nineteenth century and the beginning of this one, the poor in Norfolk farming villages were very poor indeed. Agricultural labourers worked long hours and many had large families to feed. My grandfather, Grandad Bugg, was a cowman who worked seven days a week. His father before him had been a road-mender. Grandad Bugg had left school at the age of eight. Schooling beyond eight then cost tuppence a week but there was no money to spare for that. All his life he could neither read nor write. I remember him as a lovely, quiet old man, smoking a pipe, and adored by all his large family.

As children, my sister and I never tired of asking our Dad about the family history. He had been one of fourteen children, the seventh and middle child. 'Say all their names, please!' we would cry. He could rattle off all the fourteen names at an incredible speed.

'Lily, Edie, Charlie, Bessie, Tottie, Mary, Jimmy, Ollie, Minnie, George, Ronnie, Willie, Freddie, Bertie.'

'Again! Do it again!' we would plead.

The vivid, high-speed tableau of all our aunts and uncles would flash across our eyes: 'Lily, Edie, Charlie, Bessie, Tottie, Mary, Jimmy, Ollie, Minnie, George, Ronnie, Willie, Freddie, Bertie.'

Number seven was Jimmy, our Dad. He had been born in 1899. They had all been brought up in what country people called a 'two-up-and-two-down' cottage.

'Tell us how you slept,' we used to say.

'Well,' said Dad, 'we didn't have to hang from pegs on the walls. Some of us would be four to a bed, two at the head and two at the foot. There were two beds to a room. Some of the tinier children would be in with our mother and father. Of course, our feet met in the middle of the bed, we had no pyjamas, or night-gowns – no money for that sort of thing. In the morning we used to put our feet together with our opposite number and play bicycles, toes to toes.'

Dad also liked to tell about adventures with their appletree. This is what he told us: 'When the apples were getting ripe on the tree in the garden my elder sisters would persuade me, early in the morning, to put my short shirt on and go down to get some apples. We were nearly always hungry. I would tiptoe down the stairs and go outside to pick up the fallen apples. I then had to place them on a broom-head and pass them very quietly up to the bedroom window where they were unloaded.'

'Did they ever give you any?' we asked anxiously.

'Oh, yes, I always got one or two.'

'Were you ever caught?'

'Not really, but mother would hear us through the bedroom wall gnawing away at the apples. She'd say, "What are you a-winding into you together?"'

These stories and others like them were the highlights of what is nowadays referred to as the oral tradition – the handing down of individual histories by word of mouth. Our father told of the constant struggle to feed all the hungry mouths, the usual breakfasts of bread and margarine, or bread and dripping. There would only be one slice per person. My father said that he often fainted at school after walking the mile between home and school at the edge of his village, East Tuddenham. On some days he and his brother Charlie would open their small packed lunches and finish them off, so hungry were they. Then at the proper school lunch-time in the playground Dad would hang around for any left-overs from other more fortunate children.

He told us of the Sunday morning breakfasts when his father would skilfully aim a slice of bread on to each plate spread around the table. He never missed the target. If their father had a boiled egg for Sunday breakfast as a treat, the children would wait hopefully to see which of them would have the egg-top bestowed upon them.

One of our favourite stories was about our Uncle George as a boy. It happened one summer Sunday afternoon when George was about seven years old. We loved it when Dad gave the account.

'Well now,' he would start. 'The Sunday afternoon treat was for some of us children to accompany our father as he drove the cows across the meadows to the milking parlour, as it was called, for the afternoon milking. On one occasion, George, who was wearing a hand-me-down little sailor suit, walked a little too close to the rear of one of the cows. The rich grass had enlivened the cow's stomach. The cow coughed and poor George, who was face-high to the cow's tail, got covered in cow muck. As his sisters tried to clean him up he uttered these memorable words in his broad Norfolk accent: "I aren't a gornta spit it out, I aren't a gornta swallow it. I'm gornta keep it here till the policeman come."'

Life was fairly primitive there at the turn of the century. Dad's sisters had a way of knowing when another baby was to be born into the family. One of them would be despatched to the grocer's shop to buy a packet of Quaker Oats. Their mother would eat porridge, especially for a few days before the birth, in order to build up her strength for the ordeal and for the baby's milk. The girls knew the code from previous experiences.

Before our own Christmas celebrations we might question Dad about his childhood Christmases.

'Oh,' he would say, 'Christmas was such a happy time for the family. Some of us boys sang in the church choir and at Christmas time we would walk down the church aisle wearing our hobnail boots which clattered on the grating above the heating pipes. Our short corduroy trousers would whistle, our long stockings would rub together. We would sing our little hearts out for the Christmas hymns. In the weeks before that we would have our eyes glued to the village shop windows, gazing at the decorations and the toys.'

'What did you get in your stockings?' my sister demanded to know.

'We all got the same,' said Dad. 'One orange, one sweet mouse, two or three nuts, and a handkerchief. Simple gifts, which nevertheless delighted us. There was no high living then, but at Christmas the farmer would send us a joint of meat and the village squire might send two rabbits. The chitlings from a farm pig would have been cleaned by my mother and these would have been cut up and fried. The trouble was that, due to the impoverished diet we had all the year round, our little stomachs couldn't take the rich feast. We were all usually sick after the Christmas pudding.

On Sunday afternoon, mother would read to father, who, as you know, had never learned to read, and we would overhear. She read from something called *The Sunday Companion* – mostly serial stories. She also read to him about the early days of World War I.

Some of the words proved difficult for her to pronounce.

Some of us laughed a bit when she read the word 'tuberculosis' as 'two perculiosis' and the name of a regiment called the 'Fourth Battalion' as the 'Fourth Batter a Lion'. That was one of the few occasions when father got cross with all of us children. We were not allowed to laugh at the mistakes his beloved wife made in her readings to him.'

My sister and I loved to hear the tales that our father told us. They brought to life a past which seemed to us one of almost unbelievable poverty. At the same time what shone through was the simple heroism and loyalty of our father's family. I think he was quite proud to be 'one of fourteen', as he put it. 'One of fourteen.'

Harvesting

In Shakespeare's play, *As You Like It*, some lines are spoken by Corin the shepherd which could be almost an exact description of my father throughout his life:

> I am a true labourer. I earn that I eat,
> get that I wear, owe no man hate,
> envy no man's happiness,
> glad of other men's good ...

All that my father told me about his working life and all that I heard and observed during my childhood, and till the end of his life, confirmed the picture.

A local farmer in Hethersett wanted labour for his grain harvest in the late twenties. He was a respected and well-liked man, a Mr Richardson. Now there were two ways of settling the labourer's payment for harvesting. The first fixed the wages at so much per week for however long or short the gathering of the crops would take. The other method involved negotiating a price for the whole harvest as a contract rather than a wage. The attraction of this second was that if the weather stayed dry and sunny, the work could be completed in about three weeks. If, on the other hand, there was rain and wind, with the crops flattened and days when no harvesting could be done, the men might still be trying to complete the contract by the end of six weeks for the same amount of money. It was a risky gamble against the weather. But this latter contract was the one chosen that year.

I can see my father now, sleeves rolled up, standing the

golden sheaves in sets of six. Or again lifting sheaves at the end of his pitchfork, high up on to the farm waggon. Another man is on top of the load arranging the balance so that the horse can pull the cart to the stack in the corner of the field. This may have been my first encounter with physical labour on a grand scale in a co-operative venture. How I longed to join in. I saw it all when my mother, my sister and I came to bring him the three meals a day which mother had prepared. We trekked up roads, down lanes and across fields to deliver on time for the work-breaks. These were at what was called 'elevenses', 'oneses' and 'fourses', matching the hours of the clock. The bottles of cold tea, sandwiches or hunks of bread and cheese, or meat pies, apple tarts or rice puddings all in enamel dishes were well wrapped up, and carried in wicker baskets. Apart from the long walks, I remember how the stubble of the cut corn scratched my bare legs, unprotected by my very short socks. After they had consumed the food the men rested, leaning their backs against the stooks, their heavy leather boots spread out on the ground. Some wore buskins. These were leather gaiters strapped round and over their corduroy trousers. The stubble then did not get through to their legs. After the short rest when both the men and the horses were refreshed the harvesting began again. The pace of the enterprise was unrelenting – a bit like piece-work. The faster they worked the more they would earn. The whole operation was like an open-air conveyor belt under the cloudless skies. The work went on long after 'fourses' as the daylight hours stretched out to sunset.

The summer that year was a perfect one. The harvest was finished in the record time of three weeks. The farmer was delighted, the men were paid up. The farmer then gave his permission for gleaning to start. Our family went gleaning up and down the fields, putting the left-over heads of corn and pieces of straw into sacks. We did it systematically. This time I too had long socks on right up to my knees. There was straw for the hen-houses, with grain for our chickens to eat all winter long. My father's arms and face had the natural sunburn which comes only from work outdoors in the fields. His blue eyes shone with pleasure as we carted our own small harvest home.

As I look back on it now, from a long time off, those scenes mingle with artistic representations of harvest labouring – especially Millet's *The Gleaners*. If I look at illuminated manuscripts of the Middle Ages of peasants engaged in the activities of farm life, it is always my father I see. The gold is right, the illumination is appropriate. The Luttrell Psalter rightly immortalises the age-old bonding of man with the crops of the fields. But it is only in the drawing and paintings of Millet, and Van Gogh that the true nature of hard labour is revealed.

... with grain for our chickens to eat all winter ...

A True Labourer

How had this labouring life begun? I once asked my father to tell me about his first job. This is what he told me.

'I left school when I was twelve. That was in 1912. A few of us from the top class took a special examination. I must have passed because I got a certificate which said I was ready to leave. I'll give you the exact words: "Qualified for full-time employment except in a factory or workshop if under the age of thirteen." I started work next day on the same farm where my elder brother Charlie worked. The job was stone-picking on a field. I had to pick up stones and put them in heaps all over the fields. The heaps had to be roughly the same size. I worked alone all day. When I got home that evening I told my parents what I'd done. They were upset and said I must not go back there. So I didn't. My brother Charlie told the farmer but I never heard what he said. My second job was as a copper-hole jack. A copper-hole jack was employed to do odd jobs around the farmhouse and outside jobs like lighting the copper fire to heat up the water, and keeping the fire going with wood and coal. That's where the name came from – copper-hole jack. There were other jobs like cleaning the knives and forks, sweeping the yard with a broom, pumping water up from the well, and emptying pails of rubbish. A copper-hole jack was a jack of all trades and master of none – almost the lowest form of labouring life.'

At the age of thirteen he moved up the scale to become a 'boy milk-roundsman'. The farmer provided a pony and cart which Dad drove, delivering milk to two or three villages every day. The wage was half a crown a week. The milk cost a penny a pint. He said that he called out 'Milko!' and the ladies brought milk jugs to their doors. He ladled the milk out of a large metal churn in half-pint or pint amounts.

This job lasted one year. At the age of fourteen he gained some promotion with a better wage. He worked alongside his own father who was head cowman at another farm. They milked the cows twice a day by hand and cared for the animals. This was his work for the next four years, six days a week and every other Sunday. In those four years the First World War raged in France; some of the men of the village went, never to return. Farm wages had increased during the war as food production had to be maintained. My father was away for a year in the army. When he returned he found that the farmer had recruited a Land Army girl to help milk the cows. There was no job for him to go back to so instead he joined a gang of labourers working on the roads. There was much stone-breaking and pot-hole filling to be done as the roads had been neglected for four years. The wages were very low. Eventually he returned to farm labouring. His return coincided with the time when there were attempts to reduce the labourer's wages and increase the weekly hours from 50 to 54. Feelings ran high on both sides, leading to the agricultural workers' strike in March 1923. My father told me about the events of the strike.

'Well, the local secretary of the Union became ill and no one was keen to stand in for him so I offered. It wasn't a thing I'd set my heart on doing but it had to be done. So I did it. I had to call the men from the local farms together on the village green every morning, take their names and try to ensure that the strike held. There weren't any pickets in them days. The farms were scattered about. There might be a temptation for an individual worker to 'creep back' as we said. Some went in to look after the livestock, that was part of the deal. Once a week I cycled to East Dereham to the Union Headquarters. It was seven miles away. I collected the men's strike pay, which was six shillings a week per man. I paid the men out each week on the village green and we walked around the villages nearby, explaining our case, and trying to collect money to help feed us. We had banners, and Mum pushed you and Irene in the pram. We always sang "The Red Flag" if we were collecting outside a pub. The strike lasted three weeks and ended in a sort of victory for us. The wages were not put down and the hours were not put up.'

At the end of the strike when the men returned to work my father was told by the farmer that he would not be needed. He was seen as a strike leader and troublemaker just because he had done the Union secretary's job. When the others heard this they all came away refusing to work without him. But the farmer had a way of getting round that. He gave father a fortnight's work in the kitchen gardens and forbade him to mix with the other men on the farm, or talk to them during working hours. He was 'sent to Coventry' as it is called. Once things had settled down, and the men got their jobs and wages back, the farmer was able to dismiss my father without fuss. The Union recognised that he had been victimised and paid him full wages for a fortnight while he looked for another job.

The next few years saw him moving from one farm to another, seeking work. His part in the strike had cast a cloud over his career. News spread slowly in those days but farmers talked, so that by the end of the year, when the new contracts were fixed, he found that he would be out of his job and out of our tied cottage. We would be off to yet another farm. We moved every year between my second and sixth birthday. These were the years, I think, which consolidated the deep sense of insecurity and anxiety which then affected my mother's life, with her two very young children. She faced continuous uncertainty on too many fronts. But her latent qualities of determination and natural intelligence strengthened her for the years of battling against great odds.

Dad was not a man to bear grudges. Years later he said that his part in the strike and the resulting reputation that followed him was the best thing that ever happened. It forced him to seek another occupation. He became a baker's roundsman, working in the Hethersett village bakery. With his cart full of bread, pulled by a horse, he visited all the nearby villages five days a week, enjoying this job very much. In those years I was old enough to see and know from first hand the changed pattern of his labouring life.

But there was one occurrence during the horse-and-cart delivery years which upset my parents quite a bit and was occasionally referred to in later years. One day when delivering bread to the Johnson's house on the main road through Hethersett, he tied his horse to their gatepost, which was the usual custom. He carried his basket to the back door. Just then, a car drove past and frightened the horse which reared up and shot forward, dragging the gatepost with it. For a whole year after that event Dad had money docked off his weekly wage to pay for the replacement of the gatepost. I think that he bore the unfair treatment with resignation, happy to be in a better job which he really loved. But Mum was pained by it, especially as the boss of the bakery was a prominent member of the Methodist chapel to which we also belonged. When the subject came up in later years I certainly made no bones about what I thought about the injustice done to my father and I muttered darkly about the hypocritical behaviour on the part of the boss.

A Baker's Dozen

During school holidays I went with my father on the rounds in the firm's bread van. By that time the business was motorised. I sat in the front passenger seat while he loaded all the varieties of bread on to the open shelves behind. The lovely stuff was still hot and its warm breath wafted through to where I sat. It was the smell of happiness, saturated with my father's love for me and mine for him. Certain farm smells which were powerful and all-pervading in my childhood are banked in layers in my memory: new-mown hay, the straw in stacks, manure in heaps, broad beans in blossom. After the first smells there are really no others. A new, dominant and happy smell entered my life then. It is the one smell that I would take to a desert island – my certain choice – the smell of newly baked bread.

The day's bread deliveries involved miles of travelling – it meant miles of country roads, twisting and turning, it meant farmyards, fields, streams and rivers, it meant cottages, country mansions, vicarages, and it meant welcoming country people, always seemingly glad to have their bread delivered by a man and his boy.

Once we had left the bakery in the morning we followed a prearranged route. We served the outlying places first. This was a precaution against running out of stock. It was easier to slip back to the bakery to pick up more bread from nearby. So we did Barford, Barnham Broom, Marlingford and Colney in the morning, and Little Melton, Great Melton, Ketteringham and Hethersett in the afternoon. Some of these were more like hamlets than villages in those days. We called at places with strange names like Beckhythe, The Cold Blow, The Wong Loke, Mill Lane, Kenny Wood's Loke and Old Maid's Farm. The very names of these places rang off my father's tongue like the outposts of a great empire, which for me, of course, they were.

I think he always whistled a tune as he went to the houses to announce his arrival. He carried his large wicker basket over his left arm. It contained an assortment of breads that might be needed. The names for the types of bread were equally magical for me: the cottage loaf, the Hovis, the long sandwich, the round sandwich, the little meal, the milk loaf. There were also boxes of small pastries nearer the back of the van, together with buns and cakes. These were the occasion for my learning that a Baker's Dozen consisted of thirteen cakes or thirteen bread rolls or thirteen buns, or thirteen of anything for the price of twelve – a baker's dozen.

When I first accompanied my father on the rounds I would always stay sitting in the van. I could tell when he was coming back. The clear musical whistling got nearer and nearer, followed by the opening and shutting of the back door. He would then come into the driver's seat, start up the engine and on we would go.

Sometimes in a quiet lane he would let me sit between his knees and hold the steering wheel as if I were driver. This was a peak experience. His hands were always ready to overrule mine as we drove slowly along.

When I grew a bit older, Dad provided me with a bread basket, a smaller version of his own. I delivered the simpler orders but did not collect payments. In making my deliveries I felt important and useful, trotting round, knocking on doors, letting the customers pick out their bread from my basket. Dad didn't send me to grumpy people or to those whose dogs were uncertain. I remember only lovely, quiet old ladies, lovely young ladies and grey-haired old gentlemen who would say things like, 'Are you Jimma's boy?'

'Yes,' I'd say.

'Hev yu gotta little meerl loaf please?'

When I got back to the van Dad would ask me what the folks had said. 'Hev you gotta little meerl loaf?' I'd say. 'Hev you gotta little meerl loaf?' he'd say and we would both laugh.

My father would tell me the news from his customers. Poor Mr Huggins had hurt himself at work. Mrs Bowhill's cat had had kittens; she said they'd have to be drowned. I didn't ask how, but was horrified some years later when I found out – two bricks in the bottom of a sack, kittens in, sack tied up and dropped into a pond. But, aged ten, the world wasn't real to me – there was a sort of protective veil between me and harsh reality.

Sometimes Dad imitated the wilder Norfolk accents of the more remote farmers. Old Ben Wilkins apparently said to Dad something which I could not comprehend.

'My heart alive Jimma 'bour, aren't you a gittin suffin gutty?' He referred to my father's increased weight. 'My heart alive' is a bit like 'my goodness me' and 'bour' is short for neighbour. 'Aren't you a gittin suffin gutty?' means 'Aren't you getting fat?'

'My heart alive Jimma 'bour, aren't you a gittin suffin gutty?' These and similar phrases became memorable as often quoted and smiled about. Perhaps it was the abundance of the bread which had caused my father to put on a little weight. It was freely available. Even I scraped the crumbs and broken corner bits which fell on to the wooden shelves behind my head in the van – but the loaves themselves were somehow sacred and not to be nibbled by human mice – that was understood.

The hardest days for deliveries were the ones before Bank Holidays and Christmas. Free from school I always helped at those times. There were Hot Cross Buns by the dozen at Easter and Christmas robin cakes at Christmas. And always lots more bread was needed to last over the holidays. Christmas was especially good because at that time Dad received annual gifts from some of his regular customers. These gifts were spontaneous I'm sure – no collecting box or tin, or envelope to give a hint. It was not so much the monies that delighted him, more the sign of appreciation of his service throughout the year.

These were long days. We often drove home in the dark or by

moonlight, our headlights shining on to the road ahead. Little animals would be caught in the glare of the lights and dart off into the hedge. For me, this was a pre-cinema experience of thrilling encounters and near misses. But these very long working days tired father out.

Actually, I only saw glimpses of his working life. He faced all weathers, the summer heat and the winter cold. Because he always wore a cloth cap, the hot weather made it uncomfortable for him. He was almost bald, as I remember him from my childhood. He put this down to constantly wearing a cap or hat since boyhood. But however foul the weather, the bread must be got through. Snow and ice in winter were the worst hazards – country lanes and hills were difficult. The vans sometimes got stuck and had to rescue each other. We were all glad when, a few years later, Dad's job was changed from delivering the bread to actually making it. This was a promotion to an 'inside job' as the men called it.

As an older boy, I loved to go to the bakery in the mornings and watch the proceedings. The temperature was always warm. The atmosphere was humid. There was an ever-present strong smell of yeast. In his earliest time at the bakehouse during the thirties my father and the other men kneaded the dough by hand on great wooden benches. As they pummelled the huge lumps they sprinkled white flour on to the tables to prevent the dough from sticking. Miniature snowstorms filled the air, along with the sound of vigorous thumping. The dough was then left to rise before being sliced up, weighed out and placed in the metal baking tins, ready for the oven. The ovens in those early days were fired with a coke and coal mixture. There were baker's poles with flat ends, a bit like oars for rowing boats. These were used for putting the tins into the hot oven to bake and pulling them out at the end. In those days when a baker got married, his friends made a triumphant arch of these oven poles outside the church doors for the couple to walk through.

My father worked at the bakery for the next 30 years, eventually becoming the foreman. During that time the bakery was enlarged and slowly modernised. The kneading of the dough was done in huge metal mixing bins with electrically driven spindles. The gas ovens were equipped with metal shelving. The loaves were loaded outside the oven and then wheeled in to be baked. Each new technique had to be mastered by the men. Of course there were accidents. If the gas controls were not set properly a whole oven load could be burned. If this happened it had to be thrown away and there was all hell to pay. If the bread was under cooked the bread-slicing machine would jam up and pulverise the loaves. On one occasion Dad was involved in an accident. He slipped on some fat that had been spilled on the floor and he fell against hot shelving which had just come out of the oven. His arm was quite badly burned. I can see him now, on his tall Raleigh bicycle, with one arm in a giant sling, riding off to see the village doctor. It took a few weeks to heal and when it did he went stoically off to work again. He liked to tell us how many loaves had been baked before a Bank Holiday or Christmas. It wasn't bakers' dozens, it was bakers' hundreds or bakers' thousands. If we complained that he had worked too hard he would smile and say 'Hard work never harmed no one – tha's what they say.'

WHAT MOTHER DID

Time passed slowly in my childhood. Now, in later years, it appears to rush along. In those early days I spent much time just waiting for things to happen. Time dragged, dawdled and fell asleep. Sometimes, maybe before a next day's outing or event, as Mother put me to bed at night she would say 'Tomorrow is when it will happen and the quickest way to tomorrow is to shut your eyes now. When you wake up it will already be tomorrow.' I never quite fathomed the meaning of what she had said but as I drifted into sleep I savoured the anticipation.

For six months of every year I looked forward to a great event. That was the annual Sunday School outing to the seaside – to Great Yarmouth no less. For the other six months I anticipated the arrival of Christmas. These two highlights of the year were justification for many weeks of time when only ordinary happenings filled the days.

Mother was fond of telling us emphatically that we had something 'to look forward to' as she put it. Looking forward was what life was hinged upon. For that experience I was prepared to endure a little boredom and to make use of my solitude. I learned an important lesson of life – to wait and to look forward, and to live through future happenings in the imagination. This rehearsing at leisure has stood me in good stead. It became a habit for life.

The small size of the house in which we lived provided a good reason for spending as much time as possible out of doors. Inside, our mother was always busy. Her indoor work took up a good deal of the available space. There was really nowhere else to be when she started washing, ironing, baking, jam making, onion pickling or rug making. When she did spring cleaning we surely had to get away. She often spring cleaned. It was then that most of the chairs were put upside down on the tables, with rugs and mats hanging on the line waiting to be beaten. 'You can go out and play now!' Mum would call out to us. Sending us out to play was one of the best things she could do for us.

My sister and I played hard but also worked hard. We helped with everything at home. Because we were poor, mother worked unceasingly to supplement my father's wages. She not only had to do the family housework and see to the garden. She also kept chickens. In addition she went out laundering one day a week and on another day she went out cleaning. On occasions, outdoor piece-work came along, like pea picking, brussel sprout gathering and fruit picking. Mother would be there.

There were fruit farms around the back lanes of the village. When the blackcurrants were ripe, village women, including mother, were hired to do the job of picking. They were paid so much a basket. The price was fixed so low that they needed to work quite fast to make it worthwhile. We children would hurry down to the farm after school was over. We were allowed to help our mothers as long as we didn't damage the bushes. Naturally we helped ourselves to blackcurrants – that was a bonus. But there was a limit to how many even we could eat. A checker listed the names of the pickers and the number of baskets each woman had collected.

Village women, including mother, were hired to do the job of picking ...

I can see my mother now. Her hands are purple with the juice from overripe bunches of blackcurrants, her dear face flushed with the speed and effort of the labour. It is high summer. We will go on working until the sun goes down. The smell and taste of the blackcurrants overwhelms me. I am amazed at the quantity of glowing fruit on the green bushes. The rows of baskets are gleaming in the late sunset. Mother is taking her wages and the family budget will benefit. Life, this day, is good.

Everything that Mother did was done with a high sense of purpose and a determination to do it properly. All that she tackled, from jam making, to bed making, to rockery making – she gave it her all. We could not fail to be influenced by this strong example.

Most of our clothes were homemade, certainly many of mine were. I remember the hours of fittings which I did not enjoy at all. I had to stand on the table to have my trousers lengthened or to have my sleeves shortened. The pins occasionally stuck into me and I would cry out, 'Oh, that hurt Mum!' 'Sorry!' she'd say. 'Stand up straight will you!' 'Hold your back up can't you!' 'For goodness sake stand still or I might stick another pin into you!' Her mouth was full of pins and her voice had some of the sharpness of the pins. Her scissors were at the ready.

She once acquired an unwanted suit belonging to the doctor for whom she cleaned house. It was of very good quality and had much wear left in it but it looked a little shabby. She decided that she could do something with it for Dad. Carefully, she took the suit apart entirely, turned it inside out and remade it so that it fitted Dad. He must have been the same size as the doctor. When Dad wore it for special occasions, like a male-voice choir concert, it was much admired and even envied by all around. Most of that particular piece of suit-making was carried out by Mum working on the front-room floor. We all had to tread carefully round the pieces of suit waiting for it to be assembled.

Mother was a deeply serious person. Of course that did not mean she didn't enjoy fun and laughter. But she had a quality of earnestness about her which could sometimes lower the temperature at home, unless my father's humour came to the rescue, as it nearly always did. Dad had a very keen sense of fun. I think that he and I both developed and used our cheerful natures to counterbalance Mum's rather anxious approach to life.

Looking back now, I feel sure that the making of my character and personality represented an attempt to mould together Mother's deep seriousness with Father's light-heartedness – a strange mixture. If it is true that 'what goes in with the milk only goes out with the soul', as the saying goes, then Mother as much as Father put an enduring stamp on me in those early years which will go with me right into the coffin.

Her way of saying 'I'm really vexed with you!' if and when I had done something wrong, cut me to the quick. 'I'm really vexed with you!' These are the words I seem to hear others saying, even now when I have fallen from grace. When she praised me, on the other hand, my spirits were raised to the sky.

One of her favourite poems, which she had learned and recited at her own village school at St Faiths, was one by Longfellow. She often recited it to us as children. I can hear her saying the last verse now:

Lives of great men all remind us
We can make our lives sublime,
And, departing leave behind us
Footprints on the sands of time.

She spoke it with great emotion and deep feeling, pointing its meaning directly at us. I was left wondering whether these sands were at Yarmouth, the only sands I really knew, or somewhere in the distance, like the Sahara desert. Wherever it was, I wanted to follow.

SCHOOLING

The Village School

The Hethersett British School had a bell in its small tower which rang twice a day to call us children in. The older boys took turns in ringing it. The building was of greyish stone in the style of church halls of that time. The windows were thickly frosted glass so that we could not see out. The barn-like roof seemed a long way off. There were clear windows, high up through which the light of the outside world shone down on the heads of the 80 or so scholars below. To me, as a small child, it seemed a place of giant proportions. When, as a grown-up, I visited it recently, I was amazed to see how small it really was.

At the side of the school there was a gravel playground rough enough for rough play and for playground drill. A smaller building, behind the larger one, housed the infant department. Further behind still were the outdoor lavatories. These had wooden seats at two levels – one height for infants and another for older children. Newspaper pieces hung on string from the wall. Since it was before flush lavatories, everything disappeared into a sort of cavern underground. I never stayed for long and never looked down.

As an infant of five years I began both my formal and informal education under the direction of Miss Gertie Beeby. She was no doubt a kind and gentle teacher but because she was in charge of so many of us, she appeared to be more severe and more fussy than was the actual case. She was the first adult I had come across who wore thick horn-rimmed spectacles. It was quite disconcerting to have to read what her eyes said through the shiny glasses.

I can see the classroom walls in my mind's eye. A chart hangs at eye level round two of the walls. It is a clear and colourful pictorial alphabet. The picture of an apple is accompanied by the letter 'a'. There is an orange which has a letter 'o' by it, an egg with an 'e' beside it. There are lots more of these. Perhaps I had been away when Miss Beeby had explained the significance of the charts or perhaps she had never explained them at all. I must have missed something important because I never made the connection. So for me the symbol 'a' meant a whole apple, 'c' stood for a whole cat, 'd' for a whole dog and 'f' for the whole of a fish. I was left quite in the dark about the real significance of the alphabet and never cottoned on to the fact that the letter stood merely for the first sound you made when you started to say the word.

Yet somehow Miss Beeby must have taught me to read. We had the primers of the day – full of two-, three- and four-letter words: cats on mats, mats on cats, but no tots on pots, or pots on tots. There were not many laughs around in the 1920s books. Phonics was the favoured method and strange sentences such as 'Put the pin in the bin, Win' and 'If it is in it is not out' or the surrealist example 'sit on a sod and nod to God – and me' were to be found in some of the early primers still in the back of the school cupboard.

I remember one story from my early reading. This was the fable of the Sun and the Wind challenging each other to see who could force a traveller to take off his overcoat. To my surprise the Sun was the winner. Where I lived there were often strong winds blowing and very little sun, so I had expected the Wind to be the victor. What that story really did, because of my trust in the written word, was to confirm something that I must have believed even earlier – that the sun, the moon, the wind, the rivers and trees were alive with thoughts of their own which they communicated to each other, and even to humans. They were alive, like me, only larger, stronger, more powerful and therefore quite frightening.

Dear Gertie Beeby, you led me into the life of books. It was with you also that I first smelt the unforgettable smell of newly unwrapped plasticine. My artistic life was opened up. And the sweet biscuits you handed round on Friday afternoons after story-reading before home-time – were baked especially for us. It is with you that I am supposed to be making, from cut, brown cardboard and red crepe-paper, a jester's cup and ball. I'm skipping home to Mum with it. When the paper ball is tossed up in the air it always comes back. You have told me that I have made this toy. I can't remember doing any of it, so please confess now that you did it all. I couldn't have managed it with those blunt infant scissors. I'll forgive your little white lie, if you forgive me my awkward left-handedness. How could I tell my mother that I made it?

Big School

At seven years, the inevitable move was into the big building next-door. The organisation of this school into standards rather than classes, all in one hall, would seem odd by today's practices. From the word go – the September of the year when you entered Standard

One at the far end – you could chart your progress and see the future laid out in a human diagram. No curtains, or sliding or folding doors divided the three main teaching areas. Because all the classes were taught at the same time there had to be full attention to your particular blackboard and teacher. It didn't do to eavesdrop. Everything could be overheard and overseen. I think it must have been very hard for the two young teachers, Agnes Attwell and Jessie Bachelor, to have to perform in public, side by side, with Rosie Ellis our Headmistress. This may be the reason for such a lot of quiet work, exercises in books, copying from the blackboard, silent reading, and so on.

The whole school of about 80 children would join together for some activities. The Head took us for prayers, singing and some English lessons. The singing was memorable. The songs were often sad ones, like 'Sweet Lass of Richmond Hill'. At that time I didn't know what a lass was. We only had girls. Then there was John Peel. I certainly didn't know what 'ken' meant in 'Dy'e Ken John Peel'. Ken was the name of a boy I played with. There were songs about people being so long at the fair and others longing not to be deceived or grieved, early in the morning. We sang them all in our wild Norfolk accents.

I must have shown some semblance of musical flair which Rosie Ellis noticed, or perhaps it was because I had fair hair and blue eyes that she picked me out to conduct the Standard One percussion band. I was truly surprised, I think. We had a strange assortment of instruments, a drum or two, tambourines, triangles, cymbals, and various bells. We walked round in a circle, of about ten feet across, banging out tunes like 'Oh Can't You Hear Them Coming, Dame Durban's Tin Pot Band?' That's how we must have sounded. On Parents' Day I conducted. Rosie had taught me to make an imaginary figure of four in the air, keeping time to the piano. I conducted, she played, the band banged and the parents clapped.

Another musical performance is in a play where I have to perform as Little Jack Horner. I can see myself sitting on a tall stool. On my lap I have a baked plum pie, which my mother has specially prepared. At the appropriate line in the rhyme I shall put my thumb into the pie and produce a plum, hold it high, and sing 'what a good boy am I'. But I can't get a plum on my thumb. The plums are slippery, so I go for one which has had the stone removed. I raise it in triumph but of course it collapses and falls ungracefully to the floor. My prospects for an acting career are considerably dampened.

There were other special occasions like Armistice Day. On 11th. November, at eleven o'clock, every year, we all stood up and turned round to gaze at a white marble slab high up on the back wall. There were names carved into the marble. During a long, great silence we all looked at the names. By the time I reached the top class a few years later I had many times read the names of the village lads and men who had died some fifteen years earlier in what was then called the Great War.

I think that I kept my eyes away from the memorial for much of the year. I felt that it was only to be properly regarded ceremoniously and reverently, in the great two-minute silence. But always, out in the playground, the main game for the boys was a fighting one, English against Germans, Germans against English.

On Empire Days as they were then called, parents came to see our specially prepared tableaux. About 20 children were chosen to be dressed in costumes of the countries of the Empire. The centre piece was one of the older girls dressed as Britannia with all the regalia. A child commentator introduced the countries one by one as they walked on to the stage. Objects associated with each country were also carried on by the children. This ceremony made sense of the pink colouring on our school maps of the world. All that pink on which the sun never set. Somehow we felt proud. Our collection of labels and wrappings from Empire food products served to celebrate the day. I contributed a tissue-paper orange wrapping from Spain, a sardine label from Portugal, together with a Camp Coffee bottle cover from Latin America. But, alas, these were not included in the overall display for I had unwittingly extended the boundaries of the Empire. But I still love those orange wrappers even now, wherever they are from.

Rosie also took mass poetry lessons with the whole school. We did a lot of learning by heart. Tennyson's 'The Brook' was one of the poems. It took a long time and a lot of learning. She read aloud beautifully. I can still hear certain lines that she read, especially these:

> For men may come and men may go
> But I go on for ever.

Here was an echo of 'For ever and ever, Amen' as prayed at chapel but this time set in nature.

Other lines caused me much puzzlement – in those days pupils were not encouraged to ask questions:

> I come from haunts of coot and hern,
> I make a sudden sally…

I was quite ignorant of what a coot was or even a hern – indeed I am still a bit vague about it. Coot was how we pronounced the word 'coat' in our dialect. 'Git yer coot on' we'd say. As for 'I knew a sudden sally' – I knew a girl called Sally but was mystified as to how she suddenly got into the stream.

> I chatter over stony ways
> In little sharps and trebles …
>
> I babble on the pebbles …

Of one thing I became sure – the brook was a living thing. All that talk of chattering, babbling, bickering, singing in sharps and trebles. To add to that there was talk of murmuring – these were all human activities, things even we children did.

> I slip, I slide, I gloom, I glance …

This brook, therefore, for me at least, clearly belonged to the great group of natural living, thinking, talking things that I was already aware of. The brook had an expansive powerful ego – all those lines beginning with 'I'. It addressed me personally and told me its story. Was Rosie Ellis aware of the strength of what she was handling and handing on to us as she urged us to recite in unison: 'For men may come and men may go,/But I go on forever'? The learning, too, seemed to go on a long time.

Dear Rosie Ellis, I want to thank you for your poetry. It set my heart alight and awakened my imagination. I see your face smiling fondly at me whenever I come across a brook or even a running stream. Tennyson's face comes with it. I look for coots and herns, and a sudden sally, any kind of Sally will do!

The three long years of classwork seemed to hold my attention and my enthusiasm. Tasks given us to perform were near enough to our ability, increasing in difficulty as we moved up a grade into the next standard. Each year after the summer holidays most of the class would move across the rough wooden floorboards into the benches vacated by others. Each wooden bench held four pupils so there was a warmth and cosiness about the seating. Jogging each others' elbows, either deliberately or accidentally, was a fairly regular occurrence. Cheating was helped by the closeness of our books and bodies. Not everybody moved up a class. I remember a boy whose name was Billy. He failed exams once or twice. Quite a large boy at the age of nine or thereabouts, he still sat in amongst those just arrived from the infants class. Poor Billy, he was considered the school dunce. I have a vision of him standing in the corner of the hall, facing the wall and wearing the cone-shaped hat with the big 'D' on it. In a way his plight served as a warning to the rest of us to forge ahead and not to be left behind.

The lined exercise books in which we did most of the formal work of sums and writing had very shiny covers. They glistened when they were new but quickly got battered, splattered and dog-eared, but the text printed on the front of each and every exercise book shone out clearly: 'Whatsoever is worth doing is worth doing well.' These words remained engraved upon my heart for a long time. This injunction flowed through my veins. It was like Brighton rock. As I scratched away with my thin pen-nib, and essayed the loops and tails of the copper-plate style which was prescribed for the schools of that time, I tried hard to do it well. As I blotted and splattered the ink over my short multiplications, my long multiplications, my short divisions, my long divisions, my tables and my spelling corrections, the words of the text on the front of the book echoed in my head. I respected the printed word and became a true believer. I never tore pages out of the back of these sacred books to make paper aeroplanes or write child love letters as some did. It was all so very much worth doing and worth doing well. That slogan confirmed me as a model school citizen, serious, academic, quiet and hungry for success in learning. A timid boy, anxious to please and very earnest, I think the teachers loved me, and I think I loved them. It was a great shock to my system when recently someone reported to me that he had heard an alternative version of the words of the text: 'Whatsoever is worth doing is worth doing badly' – unbelievable and heretical.

Two lessons in my second year still stand out clearly in the memory. Our teacher, Jessie Bachelor, told us the story of how the Phoenicians were supposed to have discovered purple dye. It went something like this: Phoenicians somewhere on the shore of a distant sea, walked along wearing their long pale robes. A dog of theirs ran into the waves and came out with a shellfish in its mouth. From this shell a deep purple liquid was flowing. The dog rubbed its mouth against one of the party's robes, staining it purple. The result brought a new colour into the world. What I loved about this story was that the hero was a dog, unknowing, not seeking glory, as innocent as myself, stumbling on a great discovery. If a mere dog could do that, then there was hope for me.

These words remained engraved upon my heart...

The second story exerted an even more powerful influence over me. This was about the little boy called Hans, who put his finger in a hole in a dyke thereby stopping the flood-waters from submerging most of Holland. Of course, I believed it. I believed everything. My identification with Little Hans was complete. He was my childhood hero, not Horatio on the bridge, nor William Tell with his apple, nor Harold with the arrow in his eye. I wanted to find the hole in the wall, place my finger in it and save the village or the county, or the country. At that time the sea was invading the Norfolk coastline, destroying cliffs, burying churches, flooding the fields and drowning cattle. Where was my wall? My finger was always at the ready!

Activities which came under the heading of hand-work were varied. In Standard One there were little wooden boxes containing balls of worn-out plasticine which, having lost their original colours, had turned sludge grey. We rolled these nasty little bits about on worn-out sticky blackboards. We rolled and pressed the plasticine, to soften it. Amazingly it picked up anything that was lying around – dust, bits of finger-nail, drawing pins and crumbs. I think those sessions were depressing. I don't remember if I ever made anything of significance.

Art for the next year consisted of pastel work on greyish paper. Rosie Ellis must have been given a huge pile of coloured reproductions of garden flowers. Perhaps they were from garden catalogues. There were many varieties of roses, irises, tulips, carnations, daffodils and Canterbury bells, to mention but a few. Our job was to try to make a good copy of these individual flowers. This was very difficult. Pastels were impossible for most of us – I think only one boy once managed it. The pastel smudged all over the paper and our fingers got all powdered. Even if we started at the top of the paper and worked our way downwards it was more than likely that we ended up with some kind of a mess. It seemed like it went on for ever.

One morning, Miss Bachelor suggested that we might bring in our own drawing books from home. She asked us to collect a piece of something growing on the hedgerows – a spray of leaves and berries perhaps, it being early autumn. I took my drawing book – with *DRAWING BOOK* on the cover – to school. Mother had bought this as a present for me. I found a spray of wild blackberries with reds and yellows already on the leaves. For this task we had either wax crayons or coloured pencils. This made the job easier.

My drawing book was pure magic. It was a scented one. Each page was a different shade of a pale colour and impregnated with a mild perfume. I can still smell it in my mind's nose. I can still see the beautiful spray of autumn leaves. Here was a pure and simple combination of aesthetic experiences – colour and scent combined with a more direct form of art-making. The real world had been smuggled into school. I think my love of wild flowers started then. Wild roses, field poppies, wild honeysuckle, morning glory, field daisies, all still delight me more than garden flowers. Had Rosie Ellis' shiny reproductions from catalogues put me off them for life? I still wonder about that.

A succession of hand-work activities included the use of cane to make trays and baskets. We made raffia mats, blotters and leather comb-cases which were sewn around the edges with thonging in a sort of blanket stitch. Our creations were all taken home with some pride. By modern standards they would hardly be described as creative. Was it, I wonder, peasant arts and crafts for peasant children? The skills we learned were disciplined and painstaking. The things we made had to be useful rather than beautiful. My highest achievement was a funny little wooden stool, the seat of which was made of a strange thick string in two colours which had to be curled around and woven in and out while being tightly pulled at the same time. It hurt the little hands in the making, but was kinder for sitting on.

But it was the time that we spent outside the school following various organised activities that proved the most popular. Drill time, for example, saw each class out in the playground, unless it was raining. We couldn't make much noise as this would disturb those working inside. None of us ever changed our clothes or footwear for drill. There were usually four teams. The teacher gave simple commands and we drilled like miniature soldiers. You had to know your left from your right or you would be caught out. 'Simon says, "Do this", "Do that"' trapped us in confusion. Head-turning, arm stretching, knee raising and lowering was a challenge. Marching and running on the spot kept us warm on winter days. Touching the opposite toes kept us supple in summer. But mostly it was nothing more than 'organised fidgeting'.

Team games were played in near silence. Tunnel ball was for me a real nightmare. I had to stand in my row with my head down, my legs wide apart, my hands at the ready to catch the heavy football as it came through all the legs in front of me, and then judge whether to push it along or let it go through. A lot of time was spent leaning my head on the backside of the one ahead of me. All this was in competition with the other three teams. There was great excitement every time the person at the back end of the team collected the ball and ran down to the front. Then we all had to shuffle back a foot or two. You could incur the wrath of your team in three ways: if you moved while the ball was coming through so that it hit your leg and got delayed; if you unnecessarily stopped it by picking it up to speed it on its way; and, finally, if you did not manage to stop it when you were back-boy and it rolled down to the end of the playground where you'd have to chase it. I frequently fell over from having to stand so long with my head between my legs. The girls' skirts got in the way so I couldn't see what was going on. Was it preparation for rugby scrums? The losers were always disappointed and the winners jubilant, but this was soon forgotten when back inside the school we got down to individual work in our books.

For outdoor country dancing a wind-up gramophone complete with horn was brought out into the playground. The dancing was so well choreographed with precise steps and movements of the hands and feet all in time to the music, that it made tunnel ball a light relief. The girls seemed better at it than we boys. They didn't wear hob-nail boots. Certainly my feet and hands, indeed my whole body, went wildly out of place. Being left-handed I was never quite sure which was left or right, or right or wrong. I still have difficulties. Having to grab the girl partner to swing her into place always seemed difficult. Country-dancing was one of the few lessons I dreaded and hated. It wasn't even worth doing badly, but badly I did it.

The final humiliation was the boys' juvenile sword dance. I can see the pattern of those wooden swords on the floor. We had to dance over and around them. Then, at some signal, we had to lift them high above our heads, still dancing, hit our partner's sword but not his hands or head, go round in a circle from left to right or right to left, or both at once in my case. There were inextricable muddles. Perhaps I would never be a dancer, not ballet, not ballroom, not Morris dancing. All I can do even now is a very heavy, happy, peasant-like, thumpy, one–two, one–two dance, when I tend to tread on others' toes or knock people over.

The highlight of summer afternoons was a nature walk. I cannot convey the absolute joy that these excursions gave me. Here was mystery and excitement. We walked in twos. If you were lucky it was boy and girl side by side, sometimes even holding hands. We wandered through the back lanes, following our teacher. She pointed out and named the trees, the flowers and crops. This seemed like real education in part of the real world. We usually headed towards the old gravel pit at the edge of the village. This was a favourite place, overgrown, full of wild flowers, little slopes and sand-hills. There, Jessie Bachelor would let us loose to go and collect as many different wild flowers as we could find to take back to school and do things with – like name them, take them to pieces to find the stamens, pistils, pollen, and even seeds. I cannot remember any suggestions of flowers, birds and bees having parallel lives to humans. But nice surprising things did happen. Sometimes on these walks we would find hazel nuts, blackberries and wild strawberries. Boys would surreptitiously hunt for birds' eggs, and blow them there and then, hoping not to be reported. We often got stung by stinging nettles. But we rubbed ourselves with nearby dock leaves to get relief from the pain. In all these adventures we were free to talk to each other, to call out, to show our finds to teacher and even to ask questions. It was truly marvellous to be fully alive children, a strong contrast to the subdued atmosphere of classwork inside the school, for the school was mostly a very calm place – but I can remember one violent occurrence. It stands clear and cold in my memory. At that time the leaving age was fourteen years. One of the older boys called Harold, who was the elder brother of Billy, had provoked our Headmistress, Rosie, to the extent that she took him out to give him a caning in the cloakroom where we all hung our coats and hats. We could hear the shouting and muffled thuds through the door. Harold was big and strong for his age and news reached us at playtime that he had mutinied, and had taken on Rosie. I do remember that she looked flushed and rather distraught when she came back in from the cloakroom. Her hair was ruffled. Not having witnessed the uprising or quelling of this rebel, I can only imagine a picture of this dramatic event. Who won or lost, and how, can only be guessed at. Harold was either suspended or expelled, or both. The message was clear to us all. Go to the cloakroom for your coats and hats but not for canings.

I didn't remain much longer at the school to be taught by Rosie Ellis, who for me was a revered, adored and respected figure. Having won a scholarship to the nearby city grammar school I left the British School at the age of ten and a half.

At the end of every summer term Rosie gave each child a book prize. There were no competitive prizes. We had all done whatever was worth doing (well?) so we all received books. On this last day of term, when some of us were leaving, there was an emotional ceremony in which Rosie gave us her blessing and spoke of our futures. As we collected our books we shook her hand in farewell. Some tears were shed. Through mine I thought I noticed a glistening in her eyes. My book, I remember, was called *Jack the Conqueror*. Rosie knew her scholars well.

Some years ago, in *The Spoon River Anthology* by Edgar Lee

Masters, I found a poem entitled 'Emily Sparks'. Emily, a school teacher had written a letter to one of those she had taught and who had gone out into the world. Part of its message was one that I imagined Rosie Ellis sending to me across the years:

> My boy, wherever you are,
> Work for your soul's sake.
> That all the clay of you, all the dross of you,
> May yield to the fire of you,
> Till the fire is nothing but light!
> Nothing but light!

Rosie's Letter

Rosie Ellis seemed overjoyed when I was awarded a scholarship which would enable me to go to the city grammar school. My parents were also delighted and behaved as though I had conquered Mount Everest single-handed. I did not myself feel any special sense of triumph. The reason for so much clucking, chirping and feather-fluffing from the grown-ups was more to do with the rarity of such an event. Only about once in every five years did one of the village ducklings turn out to be a swan or, at least, a cygnet.

That summer, when the names of 110 country boys and girls appeared in the local newspaper with my own name forty-fourth in order of merit, I finally accepted the fact that it was not a dream, or a case of mistaken identity. The reality bore in on me when the whole energy and interest of the family became concentrated on the project of getting me ready to start at the new school in September. There was the uniform to begin with, the red cap with its badge and gold braid; the long grey woollen socks with their red and yellow edging; the tie; the belt; the grey flannel, knee-length trousers. Added to that there were other delights – the sweet-smelling satchel, the football boots with the tin of dubbin. And on top of these were the tortoise-shell fountain pen, the protractor, compasses and the wooden pencil case. All these descended on me like gifts from the gods. Of course, in reality, my poor mother had done extra work at laundering, fruit picking and house cleaning, in order to pay for all these treasures. Money was very short during the slump of the early thirties and although Mother was full of high hopes for me, she was also full of high anxiety. I think my father wondered if they could really afford for me to stay at school until I was sixteen or whether I should be earning a wage at fourteen.

When I had been interviewed by the grammar school headmaster a few months earlier, my mother had been with me. He had asked what I wanted to be when I grew up. I replied: 'I want to be an evangelist or a minister.' That, after all, was what I told anybody else who asked the question. The chapel elders seemed to believe that I would grow up to follow some such high calling and, indeed, hadn't I already a head start in that direction? Hadn't I listened to so many sermons, prayed so many prayers, sung so many hymns and wasn't I such a good boy? I think the headmaster was surprised that this peasant lad, with a mop of fair hair and a wild Norfolk accent, should see his destiny in the pulpit. Nevertheless he accepted me for his school. Of course I never made it to the pulpit, partly as a result of the difficulties of trying to reconcile my Methodist childhood beliefs with the powerful influences of the wider world and the school I was about to enter.

The grammar school was the biggest, grandest building I had ever seen. It made the village school look like a large dog kennel by comparison. Set in its own spacious grounds, with vast playing-fields, trees, gardens, it seemed a place apart, entirely matching the grand task of bringing culture and civilisation, knowledge, and skills to the young barbarians at its gates. I knew by the end of the second week of term that this was the place above all others where I wanted to spend my days.

In the first fortnight of that year, our class met the subject teachers. We found our way through endless corridors, up and down stairs to the various classrooms, laboratories, and workshops. Our initiation was systematic and swift.

The masters wore their gowns for morning assembly. They had their uniforms and we had ours, which we wore all day, and even until we reached home at night. 'Here come Ole Red Cap', some village boys shouted when I got off the bus to go home. Sometimes it was 'Ole Big Head'. My satchel bulged with homework books, my brow was furrowed with learning.

A few of the masters at school terrified me, a few of the subjects terrified me even more, but many of the staff were gentle and their subjects attractive enough to keep us going. My form teacher for that first year was Mr Doe. His full initials were M. N. D. so, not surprisingly since he taught us English, we nicknamed him 'Midsummer Night's Dream'. He became my favourite master, teaching us with enthusiasm and inspiration. With him our set books were *The Wind in the Willows* by Kenneth Grahame and *Farmer's Glory* by A. G. Street. Midsummer Night's Dream succeeded in making these books live for me. My mother loved them too when I read pieces out to her in the evenings. Elocution was another part of M. N. D.'s work with us. Some of us were singled out by him for special attention because of our country accents. He was to help us to iron out the unacceptable roughness of our pronunciations, preparing us, as he put it, for our future careers.

The exercise I was given to perform in class, and to practise a few times a day elsewhere, was to repeat slowly 'Go home Joseph and show your nose to Rose.' The way I wanted to say it was, 'Goo hum Joosuph and show yor noose to Roose.' I don't think my parents were offended at this. They were just pleased that I was learning to 'talk proper' as they said.

All that year I sat next to David in class. We became very good friends. He was clever and lively, with a strong personality, and a great sense of humour. We both saw the funny side of lessons, and when showing excitement in class we probably laughed and giggled at times.

At the end of year one we all had reports to take home in sealed envelopes. At the lower end of the report there was a space for the form master to summarise our conduct and progress. When my parents read out to me M. N. D.'s comment, I was most surprised, just as they were. He used three words which cried out for an explanation, three words which hung over and haunted my life from then on. The words were 'lacks self-control'. My first reaction was to believe that there had been some dreadful muddle. Was it another boy's report? I was at a loss to explain to my enquiring parents what could have brought about this damning statement. However, a dark thought hovered deep in my mind. If it was not a mistake did it mean that M. N. D. had, in his infinite wisdom and profound insight, seen right through into my true character? Since then I have wondered about this many times. I seem to have spent much of my life trying to prove that M. N. D. was wrong about my lack of self-control. But sometimes I have conceded that his judgement was right. I do lack self-control. Friends have kindly said that lack of self-control is one of the best things about me. I am really good at that. So the puzzle remains.

Though I had moved to the grammar school my parents had kept a close relationship with Rosie Ellis and so my report was posted off to her in Norwich with a sorry little letter from me enclosed. Her reply dated 31 December 1934, read like this.

> Dear Eric,
> It was nice of you to send me your report. It is fairly good but I am going to give you a lecture. So sit up and take it like a man. It was rather painful to me to see that you were lacking in self-control. It made me feel that all my teaching was lost. You know that nearly all the sin and misery in the world is caused by people doing just what comes into their heads without exercising the will power which has been given them. You are now eleven years of age, quite old enough to act in a manly way.
>
> Your parents naturally have to make sacrifices to keep you decently clad and fed and it is up to you to sacrifice some of what you call your little pleasures during lesson time. It is certainly not playing the game not to make the most of your opportunities.
>
> There you are – I am not saying all this in anger, but because I want you to grow up to be a credit to me and your father and mother – so I hope you will make self-control your watchword in 1935.
>
> Sincerely Yours
> R. Ellis

The Worst of School

Unrolling a long-kept photograph of the whole school I look for the faces of my special friends – David, Bertie, Norton, Billy and Geoffrey. They shine in the polish of the summer sun. The staff are there sitting in the centre row. They look benign but with hundreds of boys all round them and above them in rows, and below them cross-legged on the grass, these adults look rather out of place, almost like a shipwrecked company marooned amongst alien tribes. These teachers strongly influenced my life in various ways. Many consequences flowed from my initiation into, and subsequent experience of, the eight or nine different studies I followed.

Mr Lamb was the chemistry teacher. His first name was Harry. Amongst the boys he was known as Black Harry. He always wore a black suit. Though his face was white his hair was black and his eyebrows thick, and for me he had a black heart. When we had first arrived at school we were warned about him by boys from the year above. 'Watch out for Black Harry,' they said. We did, for he had a reputation for being wickedly fierce and strict. He quite lived up to this reputation and I came to dread the days when chemistry was on the timetable.

My first negative experience with Black Harry concerned our first piece of homework. We were to draw and describe the parts, and workings of a bunsen burner. I had no love for the bunsen burner. As an object to depict in any fashion it had no attraction for me. My drawing was not carried out with a ruler as instructed. I represented the flame in an artistic swirl, whereas it should have been a symmetrical symbol with no individuality at all. Black Harry was merciless about it, saying things painful for me to hear and writing comments on my homework painful for me to read. He gave me a low mark.

I suppose that was the beginning of a clash of cultures between Black Harry and me. His world of science had no place for artistic vision or interpretation. From then on all the instruments and paraphernalia involved in experiments had to be drawn as symbols, not real things. Pipettes, test-tubes, bell-jars, pieces of gauze, rubber tubing were all represented in his way – thin-lined, no shadows, no beautiful ellipses even. For me they were dull and unreal. That was not the only symbolism. Water was now to be called H_2O. Until then I had loved water, seen it as precious, sparkling and pure. Every drop we used at home came from the pump at the end of the garden. For me water was water. I could not see it as H_20, two parts hydrogen, one part oxygen, and I still can't.

A frightening thing Black Harry did was on Armistice Day, which happened to fall on one of our chemistry days. He always started the lesson with a demonstration which we all stood and watched, later to record it in our books. That day he produced two tall glass jars with detachable flat glass discs at their tops. These discs were held on with thick grease. He announced that one jar contained air and the other was filled with chlorine gas. He explained that this gas was the kind used in the war and he described its effects on the lungs of the soldiers who breathed it. He then asked us to come closer and look carefully at the glass jars which stood side by side on his bench. I think he wanted us to guess which one held chlorine gas and which oxygen. As I approached the jar which I thought held the chlorine gas I felt faint with fear thinking of all he had said about the coughing, dying soldiers. I do not remember much more of that lesson. That day quite extinguished the likelihood of my ever having a love-affair with chemistry. Instead, I developed a great hatred for it. The laboratory was called 'The Stinks Lab' and for me chemistry stank.

Some boys must have liked chemistry. My friend David was very keen, but in his School Certificate year he severely damaged two fingers while making miniature bombs in his shed at home. He used chemicals and pieces of copper tubing. It was his right hand that was injured. This prevented him from sitting the exams with the rest of us and he came to school wearing a sling. I never heard what Black Harry thought about that incident.

Later in the detailed report of my School Certificate results, I note with gratification now that for chemistry I obtained a small 'f'. It says by the side – 'Symbols indicating standard reached: f= failure.'

In the first year we started to learn French and our teacher was Miss Walton. I think that she invented French Bingo and it was all played in French. Instead of numbers on the cards there were tiny pictures of familiar objects. Every week we played it during one lesson. Sitting at our desks with our cards in front of us, we tried to recognise the sounds coming out of Miss Walton's mouth: 'une plume', 'un homme', 'une pipe'. If your picture matched the sound, you called out the word and you would be given a token. I enjoyed the game. The pictures helped, but the maddening thing about French was that everything had a sex. Objects about which I had never thought in terms of masculinity or femininity now presented themselves wearing either trousers or dresses. For 'un homme' and 'une femme' that made sense, but guessing and remembering all the others was almost impossible. This system made me think that the French must be a strange people.

The exercise book we used consisted of illustrations and innumerable instalments of the life of a French family. This unending detail and description of their lives was intended to enrich our basic vocabulary but it made them seem very basic, very boring. I didn't take to them or their language. English was good enough for me, in fact I did not understand why we were learning French at all. Perhaps I was absent when the justification was given. I had heard the Bible story of the Tower of Babel and grasped the idea of people having different languages. I believed it was the fault of the French that they had a funny language. They had been on the wrong side of the Babel Tower and the English Channel.

In my first year mathematics was a deep pit. Why was it so daunting for me? Once again it was my habit of taking everything literally that made difficulties for me and particularly with algebra. I was incapable of entering a world of symbols as in chemistry. For me the letter 'x' was a letter of the alphabet. I could manage to regard it as a kiss, though to this day I do not know why 'x' stands for kiss. Is this 'x' for ecstasy, the ecstasy of kissing? I remember the teacher explaining that 'x' could stand for any number of elephants or buns or trees or cats, or dogs. Somehow I much preferred the real things, not the symbols for them. I was completely mystified. The maths teacher never convinced me of the real purpose of algebra or its practical uses. The entire enterprise seemed to be summed up by 'x = o'. Geometry and arithmetic were less of a mystery, but gave me little joy. I note on the School Certificate report another tiny symbol with a lot of meaning: 'd = weak pass'. Now that was real algebra.

Having problems with some of the academic subjects I hoped and expected to fare better in practical work. Mr Willander ran the metal-work department and Mr Bunn ran the woodwork department. Since numbers had to be small for practical work our form was divided into two. This split was organised alphabetically – the first fourteen boys went to metal-work the rest to woodwork. There was a promise that at some time in the future we would change over. To my regret that did not happen.

Mr Willander was a kind Scandinavian with a great deal of patience and very high standards. I think I started enthusiastically. There was a chance to make things. My sister, Irene, at her school, was doing cookery. Every week she brought home the results of her efforts. The family sat in judgement after tasting her rice puddings, her tapioca puddings and her semolina puddings. She was making useful things and I longed to compete. In the metal-work shop I was not put off by the iron filings, emery paper, and the oil and grime. In the two years that followed I happily filed, sanded and polished away to produce objects of use. Mr Willander demanded a perfect job. Everything had to be correct to the nearest thousandth of an inch and if polished it must shine like the sun. I think I only made three things during that long course.

The first object I completed was a flat spanner for unscrewing one-inch bolts at one end and half-inch bolts at the other. I took it home and showed my father. He was amazed by it. I don't think he had ever seen a new spanner because anything that we had was second-hand. The whole household regarded it as a thing of beauty. It was treated like a work of art, given a special place on the mantelpiece – dusted regularly by my mother. I do not remember that it was ever used or made dirty, as none of our bicycles or household gadgets had large enough bolts for it. My relatives also admired it. The spanner almost reached the realms of being a sacred object.

The second item to emerge triumphantly from the workshop was a six-inch-long cold chisel. This chisel had six sides and was made of very heavy metal. The chisel blade was sharp and dangerous. Its only uses were to break up concrete and to cut bricks in half. A side effect was to strengthen my arm muscles on account of the tremendous swings I had to give to hit it with the hammer. Several hammers lost their heads as I carved my way through concrete and brick. The chisel justified its existence because, that year, mother wanted a crazy pavement put down in the garden. The chisel was just right for that job.

My third creation was a screwdriver with a wooden handle. The handle was made on the lathe, polished with various grades of sandpaper and finally coated with linseed oil. The screwdriver lasted many years and I used it for a long time. Making a wooden handle for the screwdriver should have been the prelude to moving into the woodwork department for two years. The smell of wood and linseed had entered my nose and I longed to work with wood but alas the move never came about.

My friend, David, further along the alphabet, was on the woodwork course for two years. He had made mortice and tenon, made a pipe-rack for his father, a stool for his mother, and trays for various aunts. The look, the sound and the smell of the workshop excited me. Every time I passed the windows I practically salivated. But my Methodist up-bringing had taught me not to envy. 'Thou shalt not envy nor covet thy neighbour's handsaw, fretsaw or gimlet, nor his plane, glue-pot or spirit-level.' But I did envy them. I left school regretting that Mr Bunn had not trained me in the skills of woodworking. I was, I felt, much more of a wood boy than a metal boy. In adult life I have tried to avoid, as far as possible, all contact with iron, brass, steel, copper and lead. Silver I can manage to clean because of the aesthetic pleasure of the final polish. And gold I love.

As for my carpentry experience, I became a notorious bodger. My friends call my work 'creative bodging'. 'Never use a screw when a nail will do!' has been my motto. If I seriously wished to make my own coffin I should have to undergo special carpentry training. I understand that nails are not usual in coffins. A mortice and tenon is compulsory. The 'mort' in mortice must have some significance.

What the Poets Taught Me

One of the set books for study in the third year of the English course with my form master, Mr Doe, initials M. N. D., was *An Anthology of Modern Verse,* published by Methuen in 1921. Quite recently, I found a copy of it in a second-hand bookshop. There had been 40 reprints between 1921 and 1960. On the title page was this quotation from Matthew Arnold: 'By nothing is England so glorious as by her Poetry.' Of course, I had encountered poetry before meeting this particular anthology. Rosie Ellis had caused Tennyson's brook to flow through my ten-year-old veins, into my ears, around my skull and out of my mouth to join the mighty river with 'men may come and men may go but I go on for ever'.

At about that time, my mother had brought home a tattered book of poems along with some discarded toys given to her by one of the ladies whose house she cleaned. The book, without its cover, landed on the floor of our shed. I remember my father reading to me. He read 'The Lady of Shalott', by Tennyson. The first verse went so:

> On either side the river lie
> Long fields of barley and of rye,
> That clothe the wold and meet the sky;
> And thro' the field the road runs by
> To many tower'd Camelot;
> And up and down the people go
> Gazing where the lilies blow
> Round an island there below,
> The island of Shalott.

Though I listened in fascination to the poem, the difficulty for me was that I still had a literal approach to language, a word had only one meaning and use. We were in the shed where potatoes, onions and other garden produce were all stored. There had once been a rat in there too which Dad had chased out with a stick. Next to the shed was the outdoor lavatory. I was never quite sure where the rat had gone. I hoped far away from the lavatory, at least as far as Camelot or Shalott. Somehow we were in the wrong place for this romantic poem which Dad was reading to me. The other trouble with 'The Lady of Shalott' was that just by my nose, where I sat on the floor, were trays of shallots, a kind of onion which father had grown so that my mother could pickle them or use them to make chutney. The puzzle over these shallots, spelt with one 't' and two 'l's and 'The Lady of Shalott', spelt with two 't's and one 'l' interfered with my appreciation of the poem. An onion smell hung over the whole experience, though Dad seemed to enjoy the ballad.

If nursery rhymes, hymns, carols and folk-songs are counted as a kind of poetry then I had received a good introduction to the form. Besides, I had also written a first poem at the age of nine. This came about as a side-effect of cigarette-card collecting. In those days cigarette cards were highly prized by boys. Collecting them became an obsession, almost a mania. It was as though men existed and peopled our landscape for one purpose only – to be providers of those little cards. We stood in wait at the village slot machine. Money went in and packets of cigarettes came out. 'Please may I have the card?' 'Yes, here you are!' or 'No, I want it for my own boy, sorry.' The experience of a freshly unwrapped cigarette card, the smell of the print and the unsmoked tobacco, the crisp shiny feel of the thing, was almost ecstasy. A new card, whatever picture it bore, was superior to cards that had been out in the world for some time. A new card was not dog-eared, stained, smelling of hot boys' hands and pockets. Cards out in the world had usually been maltreated, thrown to the wall, dropped in the dust and swapped to near extinction. Eventually their front pictures became clouded and the print on the back almost unreadable. But the new card was a thing of beauty and a joy for almost 24 hours. With such a card my aesthetic life took a leap forward. I used to mount some of the cards in a small, red, shiny covered exercise-book bought from Woolworth's for three pence. On the opposite page to the card I tried to write suitable verses. Opposite a picture of a fish I wrote the following:

The fishes of the deep blue sea
When we are hot so cool can be
One day they're swimming in the bay
The next within a net they lay
But really I'd not be a fish
When all my bones lay in a dish.

The difficulty in writing poems at that age was the expectation that end words should rhyme and that there should be a rhythmic pattern in the work. This regime cramped a boy's style. Nevertheless the fish verses do reveal a premature disposition to reflect on death in the natural world and a faint recognition that the worst thing to befall a fish was death, and that this was also true for me.

When a few years later I started to read the Methuen anthology in school, it was rather like a duck taking to water. I can still recollect the impact. In examining the poems all these years later I sense that some of the foundations of my being, the very ground of my feelings toward life, were laid down in the years at school as we worked through this anthology. Turning its pages I can recognise just how and when and where certain messages about existence and the human condition first came to me, and were welcomed into my soul. That soul, as I like to think of it, was not quite the same as the one I kept in the Methodist Chapel. The mind and heart were changing too. One of the first poems in the book was 'The Little Waves of Breffny' by Eva Gore Booth. Its effects on me illustrate and symbolise the changes that were happening.

The grand road from the mountain goes shining to the sea,
And there is traffic in it and many a horse and cart,
But the little roads of Cloonagh are dearer far to me,
And the little roads of Cloonagh go rambling through my heart.

A great storm from the ocean goes shouting o'er the hill,
And there is glory in it and terror on the wind,
But the haunted air of twilight is very strange and still,
And the little winds of twilight are dearer to my mind.

The great waves of the Atlantic sweep storming on their way,
Shining green and silver with the hidden herring shoal,

But the Little Waves of Breffny have drenched my heart with spray,
And the Little Waves of Breffny go tumbling through my soul.

This short, simple poem provided a model of a way to be in a small part of the world. Hearts could be drenched with spray, minds could be haunted by twilight winds and souls could be stumbled through. I think that I must have sensed that it didn't really matter whether the place was called Breffny or Broffny or Briffny or Bruffny – any coast-line would have done, though Breffny had a more poetic sound. It could have been Yarmouth, Sheringham, Cromer or Overstrand. The main thing was to love a place with heart, body, mind and soul.

This attitude to place stayed with me over the years. Leaving Norfolk for other places was a shock to the system. It was difficult to feel in the 'Breffny' way towards places like the Elephant and Castle in London where I first lived after the war. Cut off from nature, however hard I tried I could not love the hard pavements and treeless streets, nor the crowded buildings so far away from Breffny, and the Norfolk coast.

A few pages later I found Rupert Brooke's poem, 'The Great Lover'. It seemed to follow on from Breffny almost as a confirmation and reinforcement. 'The Great Lover' widened the horizon of what could be loved. Rupert Brooke lists about 40 items in his grand confession. It included some surprises for me. He talked of 'moist-black earthen mould'. Did he, I wondered, mean the stuff I scraped off my shoes when I went indoors from the garden? Then there was the 'un-passioned beauty of a great machine'. Was this for me the great train engine standing in Hethersett station or the first combine harvester to come to the village? As for 'the strong crust of friendly bread' I couldn't make much of that. Was it the same crusty bread that Dad baked at the village bakery? How friendly could a loaf of bread really be? The most puzzling of all was 'the rough male kiss of blankets'. This must, I thought, be about the whiskers of the beards of both my grandfathers which tickled my face when they bent down to kiss me. That must be it. Rupert Brooke's occupation must have been loving everything. I wanted to become his disciple. I think he taught me to love the world.

And then I read the poem by W. H. Davies, 'Leisure'. It introduced the idea that the world was offered for more than just practical uses. It was for contemplating, looking hard at, even staring at. Three verses gave the gist of it:

What is this life if, full of care,
We have no time to stand and stare.

No time to stand beneath the boughs
And stare as long as sheep or cows.

No time to see when woods we pass,
Where squirrels hide their nuts in grass.

Unfortunately for me there was a tendency amongst older people I knew, to frown upon the non-activity of staring. They called it a waste of time. 'What are you a-gawping at?' they'd say. 'Git a moove on boy!' But my mother, when we were walking round the village, was usually content to allow me time to stare at clouds, cuckoos, rainbows and dewdrops.

When I grew up I discovered that W. H. Davies had been a tramp – plenty of time for him to stare while walking from one doss-house to another. I like to think that he might have passed through our village as many tramps did on their way from the city to Wicklewood Workhouse nearby. His poem taught me to stare and I still stare.

But it was the poems from the First World War that had the strongest impact on me. The whole horror of what had happened then was now beginning to emerge. Returning soldiers had told their stories, ex-servicemen had begged in the streets of Norwich. Collections of photographs, paintings and writings were being published. Some of these were in the school library for reference. One particular, large book of war photographs stands out in my memory. On each page there was a stark visual record of human suffering in the trenches and the mud of the battlefields. Underneath the pictures, lines from various poems were printed. I remember three quotations taken from John Keats' poem, 'La Belle Dame Sans Merci'. A wounded soldier with bandaged head stands on the edge of a shell-hole. The words read:

O what can ail thee, knight-at-arms,
Alone and palely loitering?

A photograph of devastated woods, broken trees and waterlogged fields was matched by the lines:

The sedge has wither'd from the lake,
And no birds sing.

Keats' lines served to illustrate another appalling picture of dead soldiers in dug-outs:

I saw pale kings and princes too
Pale warriors, death-pale were they all.

The effect of this combination of words and pictures was to move me deeply I had seen nothing like that before. My father had earlier acquired a six-volume history of the Boer War. In those books the artist's illustrations, which I had often looked at, were unreal in comparison to what I now saw. Photographs depicted the grim reality.

In the Methuen anthology, the first poem from the Great War, as it was then called, was Rupert Brooke's famous one, 'The Soldier'. It held a great poignancy for me, especially the first three lines:

If I should die, think only this of me:
That there's some corner of a foreign field
That is for ever England.

I knew that so many of the young men of Norfolk had gone to their corners of foreign fields. Every village memorial had their names recorded. The Great Melton War Memorial was only half a mile from our house. Round its rectangular stone base were carved the words: 'Sons of this place let this of you be said, that you who live are worthy of your dead.' In order to read all the words one had to walk right round the monument. The message bore down on me every time I went to gather walnuts at Great Melton Park or bluebells in the woods by the church. A 'son of this place' I certainly was. Something, I did not quite know what, was expected of me. How could my worthiness be tested? That was the question.

My habit then of placing all the literature I read in my own landscape, giving it a local habitation, meant that Rupert Brooke's corner of a foreign field was the field at the top of our garden. A hole dug in the corner of this field had none of the heroic overtones of the rest of the poem, such lines as 'In that rich earth a richer dust concealed.' What we dug up was clay and stones, worms and roots, bits of broken glass, and rusty metal. It was the first three lines that I concentrated on and got stuck with. In the school library pictures of battlefields, graveyards and war cemeteries had taught me that there were some corners of foreign fields that were not only for ever England, but for ever France, Germany, Belgium, Canada, Australia and New Zealand. The soldiers all had their corners. Part of me believed that was all they had.

Towards the end of the anthology, since the poets were arranged in alphabetical order, the name of Wilfred Owen appeared. Up to this time I had thought Wilfred to be a silly name. That was the name of one of the characters in a daily newspaper comic strip of the time called *Pip, Squeak and Wilfred*. For me Wilfred was the really silly one, so I wondered how anyone named Wilfred could do anything worthwhile.

There were three of his poems in the anthology: 'Miners', 'Anthem for Doomed Youth' and 'Strange Meeting'. I think that these three poems, more than anything else, conveyed to me the immense tragedy that had happened only a few years before my birth. These poems almost overwhelmed my thinking and feeling during adolescence. Sadness and despair were the dominant moods inspired by them. In the poem 'Miners', it was not a corner of a foreign field that was the soldier's destination – but the depths of a burnt-out coal-mine.

> And I saw white bones in the cinder-shard.
> Bones without number;
> For many hearts with coal are charred
> And few remember.

Even now, the last verse of 'Miners' makes me reel.

> The centuries will burn rich loads
> With which we groaned,

Whose warmth shall lull their dreaming lids
While songs are crooned.
But they will not dream of us poor lads
Lost in the ground.

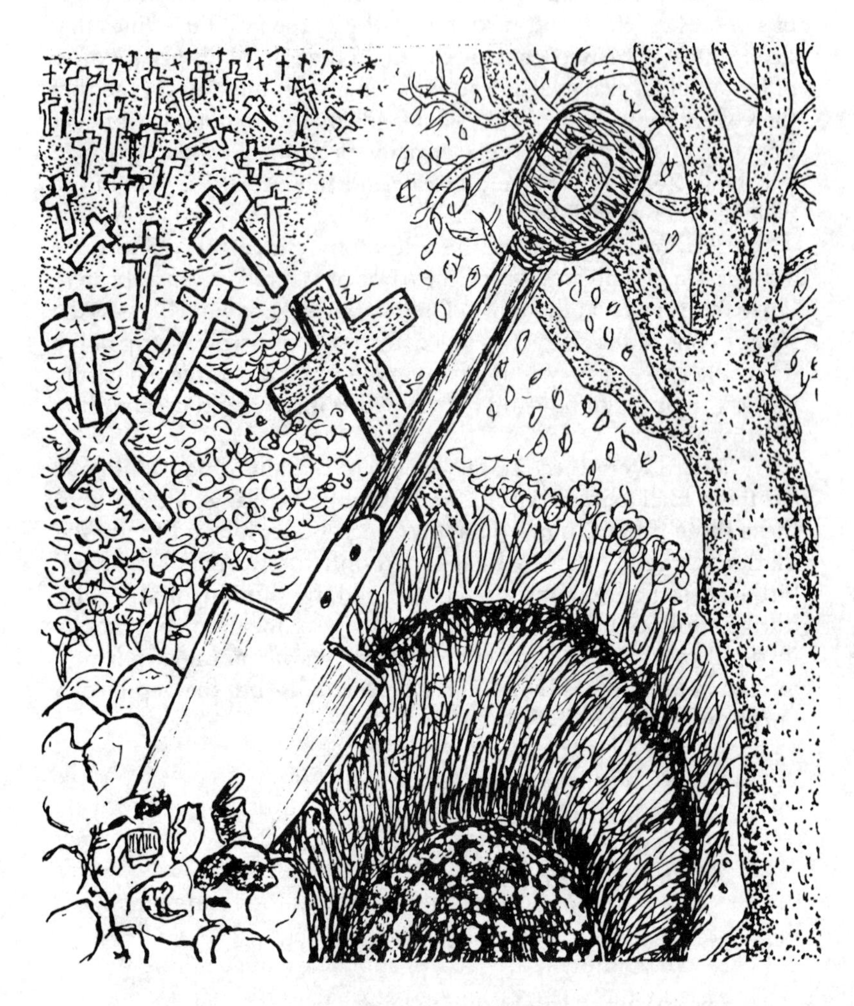

What we dug up was clay and stones, bits of broken glass and rusty metal ...

So, by my fourteenth year, I had learned that war was a corner of a foreign field, a burnt-out coal-mine and the vast hall of hell. The despair which I have spoken of was not caused by any conscious awareness of the likelihood of yet another Great War to come, though at home there was talk of a new war but a hope that the League of Nations might prevent that happening. People began signing pledges renouncing war, but somehow the thoughts of death and the uncertainty of the time of its arrival held great sway in my mind. I think that much of the poetry in the Methuen anthology initiated me into a tragic sense of life which has never quite left me. Perhaps I was too young to meet what one poet, W. W. Gibson, calls 'The heart-break in the heart of things'. Was this possibility of a gloom-laden life all that I was meant to gain from the poets, all that could be offered to a lad at the outset of his life? I have often wondered whether the others in my year at school took it all as seriously as I did. Had they perhaps been warned that a little poetry goes a long way, in one ear and out of the other. Perhaps they let it wash right over them. I just drowned in it. But coming up for the third term I did find a short poem to grab at and gain solace from. It represented a way of escape. It was, of course, W. B. Yeats' 'The Lake Isle of Innisfree', a famous and much-loved poem. Here was the best antidote to despair. All that was needed was a log cabin, nine bean rows and a beehive. 'To live alone in a bee-loud glade' in Innisfree, was the answer to everything. 'I will arise and go now' I used to murmur all over the place. When things get tough, even today, I murmur the lines. 'I will arise and go now'. Go somewhere, go anywhere. I will arise and go.

The Play's the Thing

My favourite teacher, M. N. Doe, did not deserve his nickname, Midsummer Night's Dream. There was nothing dream-like about him. But the name was appropriate in so far as he produced the school play, *A Midsummer Night's Dream*, performances of which were for the school and the public. It was during my third year and he chose me to play Bottom. I think that, in his judgement, my Norfolk accent suited the part.

Older boys in the art department made a huge donkey's head, constructed from wire netting, papier mâché and bandaging, and with a movable lower jaw which could be pulled up and down by a string hidden in my costume. I remember trying it on while two of the boys located my eye positions with pencils to provide a look-out for me.

M. N. D. supervised all the rehearsals, instructing us how to act, move, project our voices and use our hands for gesturing. While wearing the ass-head at the performances there was no holding me. It was warm inside the head. I felt a bit enclosed but managed to yell my lines out through the donkey's mouth while wagging the jaw in time. I could hardly see anything through the two small slits made for my eyes – could barely see the fairies and just managed not to fall off the front of the stage while singing my song. As for Titania, I did not want to look at her in any case. What was Tom Roberts doing reclining on a grassy bank, dressed in a long, flowing gown, his face powdered white, his lips stained scarlet and on his head a wreath of flowers? I was truly amazed and shocked at the transformation.

In the Pyramus and Thisbe comedy at the end of the play I was supposed to stab myself with a sword. The lines gave me problems.

> Out, sword, and wound
> The pap of Pyramus;
> Ay, that left pap,
> Where the heart doth hop ...

Being naturally left-handed I was inclined to being right-hearted. Consequently I sometimes hit the wrong pap with my sword in the wrong hand. In the end M. N. D. said it didn't really matter that much.

I have always been glad that I was given the part of Nick Bottom, the weaver, not Snug the joiner, Robin Starveling the tailor, Peter Quince the carpenter, not Francis Flute the bellows-mender. To have been Tom Snout, the tinker, would have been the real humiliation. Somehow I think that if I had not played Bottom my life would not have been quite the same.

I find it odd that something of 'bully bottom', the 'rude mechanical', the 'hempen home-spun' has remained in me ever since. One of my oft-used phrases has been 'Here, let me!' In this willingness to volunteer for almost everything I detect an echo of Bottom's wish to roar like a lion, coo like a dove, play the knight and play the lover. At the same time he had the practical imagination to solve problems. 'You want a wall? Here is how to do it! You want a moon? This is how!' That aspect of his character has always appealed to me – the capacity for instant problem-solving, even if the results are bizarre or even outrageous. He was fearless, he lacked self-control and was a generally exaggerated being, a man of great enthusiasm, optimism, and egotism. He thought he could do anything and everything. Bottom was clearly something of an ass even when not wearing the ass-head. Some of these manifestations I have occasionally observed lurking in my own character. Had M. N. D. spotted the hints of a resemblance when he picked me for the part in 1936 when I was fourteen? No doubt I got into the character while the character got into me.

Perhaps we should be careful about which parts we play in adolescent drama for, as Plato maintained, drama is powerful stuff which exerts strange influences. I seem to recall that my friend David played Lysander. His love life in the real world began earlier than mine with interesting complications that would not have surprised Shakespeare.

On my school-leaving report, which I still have, the Headmaster has written: 'Acted Bottom in the Dream with great vigour and success.' Was that intended to be a recommendation or a warning to potential employers I wonder? Alas, there was little chance to find out, for, at the age of sixteen, I took my first job as a junior clerk in the County of Norfolk Taxation Office. A far, far cry from the enchanted woods of Athens.

At school it was difficult for me to grasp the whole structure and complicated plot of *A Midsummer Night's Dream* while we were studying it. But the passages we learnt by heart and had explained to us by M. N. D. left me with the feeling that the play was really set in Norfolk, not in Athens, or anywhere else in England or Greece. I set the play in the only landscape I knew. Titania's speech beginning 'These are the forgeries of jealousy' where she goes on to list the devastations wrought to the seasons and weather by her quarrel with Oberon. These could match our village in part:

> The ploughman lost his sweat, and the green corn
> Hath rotted ere his youth attained a beard;
> The fold stands empty in the drownéd field
> And crows are fatted with the murrion flock;
> The nine men's morris is filled up with mud,
> And the quaint mazes in the wanton green
> For lack of tread are indistinguishable.

This could almost be Hethersett in a bad season – our cornfields, our sheep-folds, our drowned fields, our village green with mud everywhere. Shakespeare must have been there. If Jesus could walk upon England's mountains green and be on England's pleasant pastures seen, surely Shakespeare's feet in ancient times could have been by my Running Stream. He knew the bank whereon the wild thyme blew, where oxlips and the nodding violet grew. He could have known the giant oak tree in the Running Stream meadow.

The year after the school performances of the play M. N. D. read us Sonnet 73:

> That time of year thou mayst in me behold,
> When yellow leaves, or none, or few do hang
> Upon those boughs which shake against the cold,
> Bare ruin'd choirs, where late the sweet birds sang.

My Running Stream oak tree became the one where I entwined all the words of that sonnet in thin air. Whenever I return to the village I walk down the hill. The oak is still there and for me the words are still entwined in its branches.

M. N. Doe was the teacher who had written 'lacks self-control' on my school report in 1934. This remark had worried and puzzled Rosie Ellis, my parents, and myself. I had, after all, been so well behaved, amenable and anxious to please until that time. Was it the company of high-spirited companions in the boys' school that had lifted the lid allowing some lack of control to emerge? I had never really understood the significance of it until, quite by chance, I met M. N. Doe again in 1990. It happened when I was on a visit to Hethersett from London. My brother-in-law, Donald, told me that Mr Doe was in Hethersett Hall, a Residential Country Nursing Home, just a few minutes walk away from where I was staying. I became very excited and immediately decided to walk over, and visit him. Fifty years had gone by since I had last seen him. I tried to imagine him now as a ninety-year-old man.

As I entered his large room, I saw him seated in a deep armchair, a frail and delicate figure. I recognised his fine face, though, of course, he didn't recognise me. I explained who I was and we started to reminisce. This led me to remind him of something he had done for me: 'You helped me to modify my Norfolk accent.'

'Did I really?' he questioned. 'Was it "Go home Joseph and

show your nose to Rose?"'
I laughed. 'Yes, it was my wild Norfolk "o"!' I said.

'My goodness, we wouldn't do things like that today, would we?' he said, and we both laughed.

I then brought up the subject of 'lacks self-control'. He found it difficult to think of an explanation for this comment. I then laughingly told him that it had almost become my motto in life! Reminding him that I had sat next to my friend David in class, and that we two boys had giggled and laughed a lot together during lessons, I suggested that this could be the reason.

'Yes,' he said, 'perhaps that could have been the cause, though why laughter should have been something to disapprove of I cannot imagine. I fear there is not enough laughter in the world.'

I was happy at last to have the true explanation. I asked him if he had known our nickname for him had been Midsummer Night's Dream.

'Of course I did,' he said. 'I wrote it clearly on the inside of my leather briefcase; teachers know much more than their pupils suspect.'

I went on to tell him what his reading of Shakespeare's Sonnet 73 had done for me: 'I have to tell you that every time I come back to Hethersett, I visit a certain oak tree by the Running Stream and remember your reading, together with the explanation you gave of its mystery and meaning. That particular tree is very old now. Branches fall off it every year or so and it has become a sorry sight, but my associations of that tree with that sonnet and with you have stayed vivid, taking on deeper meaning as the years have gone by.'

He nodded. 'Isn't that strange,' he said. 'Do you know, I've got a tree as well. You see that large oak at the end of the garden? Well I sometimes recite those same lines to myself. It's still a good strong oak.'

He seemed surprised and moved by the warmth of my appreciation and praise for his teaching.
'It may have been what you as a child brought to the lessons. You must have been receptive from the start,' he said kindly. But I knew that it was his own sensitivity and imagination as a teacher which had illuminated the poetry for me. And so I told him.

At that moment, the staff of the home were waiting to take him to lunch, so I thought it best to leave them. I waved goodbye to him at his door.

A few months later M. N. D. died. When I heard the news I

was upset. Amongst other memories of him, I recalled how he had introduced us to Jaques' speech – 'All the world's a stage' – from *As You Like It*. I remembered the mirth caused in the class by his reading of the lines:

> And then the whining school-boy with his satchel
> And shining morning face, creeping like snail
> Unwillingly to school ...

The other ages and stages of life meant less to us then, but we certainly appreciated the school-boy one.

The news that M. N. D. had left the world's stage saddened me. He had departed, 'Sans everything.' Perhaps I had been one of the last of his old pupils to visit him – late, but not too late.

The words are still entwined in its branches …

THE OTHER SEX

It is difficult for me to recall just how early in life it was that I first recognised that there was an essential difference between boys and girls. The obvious external signs of contrast were that we boys wore the short trousers, and the girls had skirts or dresses. I was not curious about what went on underneath this clothing. But I realised that a distinction was made when it came to school lavatories. One door was for boys and another for girls. The rigid application of these territorial zones suggested to me that enormous significance was attached to certain mysteries which were only revealed in privacy behind the clearly marked doors.

A non-reader had to be very careful. Symbols were not used in those days – the words 'boys' or 'girls' had to be recognised. Dreadful things might happen to a boy if he went through the wrong door. The difference behind the doors was not only the plumbing, which was primitive in our school, but a whole way of life hovered around these two simple door signs.

The main thing which I think I noticed at quite a young age was that girls were generally kinder than boys. Other boys would thump me, wrestle with me, hold me down on the ground for three counts or ten. They might throw stones at me, take away my toys or be unusually rough. The girls I met and played with then were gentle. The facial differences were quite noticeable. Boys grimaced, grinned, laughed and shouted at each other. But the girls smiled; their voices were softer; their hair was longer; their eyes seemed to contain less menace. What for me was a more or less instinctive fear of the other seemed to fade when I was with girls. I would not be beaten up, pushed into the mud or the nettles. Most of them were weaker than me, in contrast to the boys, who all seemed stronger, always wanting to use my body just to prove their superior strength.

At the village school when I was seven years old, one of the first games I encountered celebrated the boy–girl distinction by pairing us off into what was called 'sweethearts'. I thought the word was beautiful even then. I am not sure how this ritual was initiated or how its popularity as a game spread. Pieces of paper about two inches wide and eight inches long were surreptitiously prepared by scholars under their desks in school. Lists were written on one side of the paper of all the available girls in the class. Other lists showed all the available boys, usually about a dozen. The lists were then

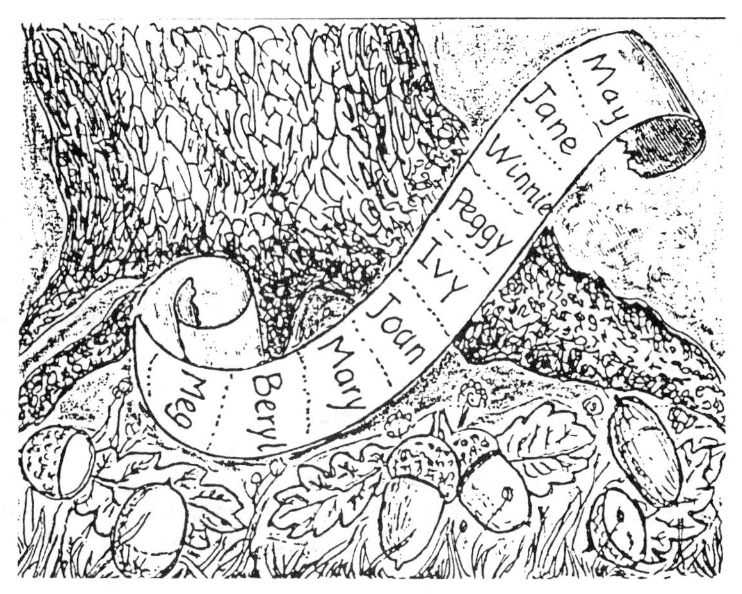

The exact spot was under a big oak tree ...

rolled round pencils leaving just a tab sticking out at the end. All names were well hidden. On the way home to dinner a girl advanced towards me holding a rolled-up list in an out-stretched hand. I was invited to pull the roll and leave my finger at a random place. Where my finger stopped my destiny began. I remember very clearly the first sweetheart to whom fate had assigned me. Her name was Ivy – I have long forgotten her surname. The exact spot was under a big oak tree a few yards from the school – there were acorns on the road. It was the kind of tree King Charles had hidden in but he wasn't there now. I cannot picture this sweetheart in my memory – she is lost too – but as the words 'Ivy is your sweetheart' were pronounced, and as the roll of paper was taken from me, I felt a childish elation. The surprise of this happening, how open it was to chance, the odd matching of name with finger, the power of the ritual quite stunned me. I did not yet know what a sweetheart really was but I went home to dinner knowing that it was only good.

Some boys groaned when the name of a girl was read out to them: 'I'm not 'avin 'er! Gimme another go.' Some girls groaned when the boy's name was read to them – 'Oh no! Not him!' but they were a little less choosy than the boys. Of course no action followed these listings. The lists themselves fell into puddles or dropped down drains – there were no contests, no duels. But to be sweethearted was something to be glad about. It was simple, innocent, and harmless as a game of noughts and crosses.

A more complicated and sophisticated way of finding a sweetheart involved a paper folded up in many ways which, when you said a number or a colour, opened up like a duck's beak. The paper kept on quacking at you until in the end it revealed a girl's name. All these rituals were a rather heady mixture bound to lead to disappointment. I never succeeded in obtaining the actual embodiment of the proffered sweetheart – only her name.

A much more basic, but still accidental, confrontation with the other sex occurred on wet playtimes when Rosie Ellis and the other two mistresses went away to have their tea, or coffee, in the usual fifteen-minute break. On wet days we children stayed in the building. When I was eight coming on to nine years old I took part in a game we called 'benching'. Our benches were about six feet long, where we normally sat for lessons. If slightly moved they could be used for other purposes. The seats were shiny and slippery, wide oak planks. We could sit astride these benches as if on horseback with our legs down on either side. The activity consisted of some of us boys and girls sitting one behind the other at one end of the bench, facing towards the centre. At the other end there was an equal number facing towards the middle. At a given signal, we slid along to meet each other. Each team had to push as hard as possible. The theory of the game was that one team would push the other off the bench. Here began my first realisation that theory and practice may not always match. The significance was really for the two facing each other in the middle, usually a boy and a girl. As the ones behind pushed, these two were almost crushed to death in a full frontal embrace. This was considered by many to be a great excitement. I do remember being piggy in the middle and falling off the bench breathless with the girl who'd been shoved down the bench towards me. The sliding about on the benches was a challenge to one's stamina and capacity to resist suffocation. The lungs must have been strengthened. I doubt whether other parts were damaged. The basic nature of the game was certainly an advance on the abstract process of name choosing. But there was no real free choice. I was just pushed into the arms of any random girl sent flying towards me. It was very exciting.

But life provided other occasions where, in peace and quiet, a boy could make his own decisions, and not be a victim of chance or the herd. At the age of nine or thereabouts I think I made a conscious choice about another Ivy. This one was Ivy Spooner. My parents took my sister and me to visit the Spooner family in East Tuddenham. My sister, I think, liked Ivy's brother Kenneth. As we all played together Ivy must have smiled at me and I must have smiled back at her. It was summer; we had been playing ball in a green meadow. I had taken off my white woollen pullover because of the heat. She lent me a handkerchief to wipe my sweating forehead and offered to look after my pullover. At that moment, when I looked at Ivy, I had a strange sensation, just below the heart, but just above the stomach. It was, I believe, the first manifestation of something very much like love. Ivy and I did not have much conversation that day but we looked at each other. She smiled, I smiled back. My sister, maybe for her own ulterior motives with the brother, pronounced us sweethearts, and I felt sure it was true. The odd thing is that, ever since then, whenever I have fallen in love, the strange sensation around the region of my heart has been the sign – the state of being truly sweethearted. I know of no more reliable sign.

During school spring and summer holidays village boys and girls roved around the fields and hedges playing country games as old as the hills. We loved to climb trees, haystacks and the insides of barns. Across the fields from our home were the old cart sheds. In these falling-down buildings were old horse-drawn farm carts, not often used for harvesting. They stood very tall and there were high sides to climb over. The cart sheds were dark at the back but the front ends of the carts faced into the light. A few boys and girls clambered up into these carts, myself amongst them. There was plenty of straw there with which we pelted each other. I remember that once the games really got going I was put up into the driver's seat beside the whip for the horses. I was up there to drive imaginary horses and perhaps to keep a look-out too. I was much younger than most of the others. I drove my stationary horses with great zeal. I had been instructed never to look round behind me but to just keep driving, so, being an obedient child, I did as I was told. I listened to the sparrows in the eaves and the pigeons cooing in nearby trees. I suppose I wondered what the boys and girls in the back were doing. Was it some version of 'mothers and fathers' that I did not know about, or another favourite game, doctors and nurses? There was much giggling and laughing behind there. They'd had a lot of fun and much rustling of straw. Eventually they all climbed out and down the wooden wheels with straw in their hair. I was lifted down but nobody told me that I had driven well.

Another game which gave me some insight into rituals that might have been enacted at the back of the farm cart was played indoors at our own home. My sister Irene and I were often left in the house while our mother went to do washing or cleaning at various houses in the village. Irene was ten years old. I was eight. On some of these holiday mornings a girl about the same age as myself came to our house while her mother also went out washing, ironing or cleaning. I think the girl's name was Joyce. I quite liked her. We played 'schools'. My sister Irene was the Headmistress, Rosie Ellis. She was pretty fierce in her imitation of Rosie. Joyce and I were given school tasks to perform and worked away at them while Irene trounced us for bad behaviour, cheekiness, or stupidity. Half-way through the morning Irene rang a little toy bell and told us we could go out to play. This meant that she would stay in the living room eating biscuits and resting while we went into the kitchen. The doors were closed. Joyce and I were alone. What the playtime games were meant to be I never really comprehended. But it always seemed to be wrestling, with me on top of Joyce on the coconut mat by the outer door or Joyce on top of me on the coconut mat. At times we were in a half-way position, fighting for dominance. For me this was not quite like wrestling with a boy – there seemed to be a subtle difference. We wrestled away animatedly but in my being I felt uneasy. Whatever it was it should not be happening.

One playtime the worst happened. Mum came back early from her work, she pushed the back door open, and almost trod on Joyce and me huddled down on the coconut mat. Her face seemed a long way off as she looked down and said 'What ever are you two doing down there?' Irene, with apt presence of mind, quickly opened her door to say that it had been school playtime and we had been wrestling and having a pretend fight. I expect we children blushed. Mother either knew or she didn't know. Nothing more was said save that in the future school playtimes must happen outside the house and not inside.

I think that it was in my twelfth year that the ultimate significance of the differences between male and female was suddenly revealed to me on the top field by Dan Dewing. We were lying in the thick grass one summer afternoon, chewing blades of grass and looking at the sky. He suddenly said, 'I know where babies come from.' Dan was a quietish boy, a year older than me. His revelation of the facts of life to me took about half a minute from start to finish. I did not ask him to tell me. He just forced the knowledge on to me. Perhaps he did not want to keep it. The story went something like this, in his words: 'Your father puts some eggs into your mother's stomach and they float about there a long time – about nine months. His eggs get mixed up with her eggs and turn into a baby.'

I was thunderstruck. I did not wish to hear any more. Unfortunately, the knowledge that his elder brother had given him and his garbled version of it failed to specify what kinds of eggs were involved. The only eggs I knew about were birds' eggs or chickens' eggs. But the prevailing images that Dan left me with in that short summary was one of fried eggs. I could see these two eggs just as they looked in a frying pan. They splashed around in something like a small version of the Milky Way or a nebula shape. All this, Dan swore, had happened before I was born, all in my mother's stomach.

I had spent eleven years of my life in splendid innocence, or ignorance, not guessing that the birds, bees and flowers hinted at a deeper truth, more bizarre, more bewildering, and closer to the farmyard than the heavens. When Dan finished his short oration it was teatime. The chickens in our garden were clucking. I never felt quite the same way about fried eggs again. Of course, I told nobody of my secret knowledge but pondered it for many days.

The chapel was still the place where I attended and worshipped, and when I was about thirteen, a new, quite large organ was acquired. It had bellows which needed pumping by hand and I was appointed unofficial pumper. Sitting at the far side of the organ I pumped happily for the hymns, the offertory and any other music that was played. People seemed pleased with the way I did it. One advantage of this job was that I could see the entire congregation, see who came in late, who fell asleep during the sermon and see all the flies swirling about on the back windows. I spent a good deal of the time looking at certain girls to whom I was attracted. I hoped to catch their eyes and give them half a smile, and wait for one in return. I must have been doing this rather whole-heartedly on one occasion and did not manage to pump the bellows hard enough. The organ spluttered, made a downward whirring sound and the organist looked over to me in great alarm. The hymn faltered and went limp.

Speeding up the pumping, I blushed to the roots of my hair, hoping that my failure had not been seen to be connected with my roving eye. Sadly, a year later, an electric pump was purchased, and installed, only needing to be switched on and off. My services were, alas, no longer necessary.

The chapel Christmas parties were eagerly looked forward to. The Sunday school hall was large and bright with Christmas decorations. After a bumper tea party we played games like 'winking'. For this game, chairs were placed in a circle facing inwards leaving one chair empty. A boy stood behind each chair, the girls sat on the chairs. The boy behind the empty chair then had to wink clearly and deliberately at one of the seated girls. All the boys hung on to the shoulders of the girls in their chairs who feigned or really tried to respond to the lonely, winking boy. There was confusion, misdirected winking, embarrassment and loud silences when the fall of an eyelid could almost be heard. The really exciting thing for us, I think, was the chance to handle and be handled by the opposite sex, dressed in our best clothes as we were on those days.

Winking was fairly tame when compared with 'Postman's Knock'. For this each child had a number and we all took turns at being postman, when we had been called out to collect a delivery. The postal delivery took place in the small entrance hall which had a large coconut mat and a big, strong door. Most times when I had played this game nothing unusual had happened. A girl got your number or you got hers. She gave you a peck on the cheek out in the little hall. You gave her one back. Sometimes we might try to kiss on the mouth but we usually missed target, or hit noses and teeth with a clash.

But this particular year at the party some girls from the city had come along with their local cousins, perhaps as guests. They were not genuine Sunday schoolers, I think. Soon my number was called out. I was to receive a parcel with three stamps on it. I trooped off into the dark little place behind the hall door. There a tall, strapping thirteen year old descended on me, took hold of me and kissed me firmly, three times on the mouth, as I had never been kissed before. That was the three stamps. She then put her tongue right into my mouth. That must have been the parcel delivery!

I was utterly startled and taken aback by this strange invasion. Having my own tongue in my mouth was quite enough for me. The feeling was like a warm, melting, tasteless ice-cream lolly coming for my throat. I've never ever forgotten the experience. I told no one about it and have kept it as a closely guarded secret for most of my life. The fact that it was in the chapel Sunday school, that God might have seen it happening, added to the shock of this event. Later on, I heard adults say of certain city girls: 'She's quite a parcel!' Was this the 'Postman's Knock' connection?

However, that experience did not prevent me from being interested in girls, especially certain chapel girls and especially when I was allowed to wear long trousers for the first time. My sister was friends with some of these girls, with May and Mary, with Peggy, and Joyce. From amongst them I liked Mary most and walked round the lanes of the village with her on Sunday afternoons and evenings. Mother always invited the girls home to tea for she was keen to appraise them. But she need not have had any worries. They were all as good as gold. Our relationships were quite innocent. The afternoon walks were round Kenny Wood's Loke and through to Kissing Alley – a tree-lined, bush-lined pathway on the edge of the village. The name Kissing Alley suggests amorous prospects, but we did no more than talk earnestly, looking into each other's eyes and leaning over the gates of fields.

But Sunday evening walks were a little different. The darkness which I had earlier feared and complained of, now came into its own. The moonscapes, starscapes and the frequent pitch blackness which had surrounded me at night as a young child were now the very best surroundings for wandering out with my favourite girl. The absence of street lights was a clear advantage. The darkness which had previously distressed me was now a kindness. It hid our hand-holding as we stood under the great oak trees, leaning against their rough bark. It shrouded the goodnight kiss by the gate. And so I finally came to forgive the village darkness, came even to welcome it, love it, and treasure it.

I walked as usual down to the Running Stream ...

WORDS TO END WITH

My heart's a coffin cold
In which my Childhood lies
Unburied yet; and will –
Until this body dies.

The tramp-poet W. H. Davies said it long before I came to realise its truth. What 'lies unburied yet' for me stays on with undiminished clarity. In setting it down I tried to resist the appeal to romanticise, but of course rose-coloured spectacles do give glimpses of remembered happiness in a little paradise. As for the sadder, and grimmer occasions, they can be relived and treasured too as part of a whole life. A wise man said 'life must be lived forward but understood backwards'. What emerged finally enabled me to make some sense of my childhood's place in relation to my many years of adult living. The sad–happy, strange mixture had contained all the ingredients for the formation of my particular character and being.

The village community of the twenties and thirties played its part too. It functioned helpfully on the side of children like me. The size of the place was just right. There was plenty of open space for us to wander in, well apart from the grown-ups' activities and there were chances for us to carry out our adventures on the edge of their more important pursuits.

When children and grown-ups joined together for village occasions – horticultural shows, harvest festivals, Sunday school outings, choir outings, faith suppers, fêtes and firework nights – an atmosphere of genuinely shared enjoyment prevailed. I remember mostly kindness and tolerance from the adults I knew in those times. The village was small enough for us all to know each other. But perhaps the only division in village life that impinged on my growing up was of church versus chapel. For us children it meant that if your parents were church you went to the National School and if they were chapel you went to the British School. This inevitably led to rivalry and childish enmity which it was difficult to grow out of.

On my last visit to Hethersett I walked as usual down to the Running Stream. It was January. The leaves had fallen off the old oak tree. There were just bare boughs. That year my mother had died on her ninety-fourth birthday – she had outlived my father by twenty-one years; my sister Irene had died suddenly a few months before:

three of my close family gone, leaving me bereft and feeling sadly alone. Most of the older village folk that I remember from my childhood have also made their exits one by one.

Of course, the village has changed beyond belief. The human population has increased fivefold since the thirties. The farm animal numbers have probably diminished fivefold. There are more new houses and bungalows than old cottages; fewer barns, cow-sheds, pigsties and hen-houses. Progress, however, is confirmed by the presence of street lights, four schools, a large library and a bank. But as with most villages, its ancient origins and history have not disappeared. The heart and character of the place live on in altered times.

Several years ago when the University of East Anglia was about to be built at Earlham some three miles away from our home, my parents told me with some pride that they had made a contribution of the price of a brick or two towards its building – altered times indeed, and the coming eclipse of a once rural scene.

But in my head I still carry the images of the Hethersett of the thirties, and at night I often dream of it exactly as it was then – a beautiful and benevolent pastoral setting, just the right place where a country child could grow up.

It hid our hand-holding under the great oak trees…